BEING A FIRST AID KIT

SHAVETTA CRAIG

For information on the content of this book,
email: shavettacraig42@gmail.com

JMPinckney Publishing, LLC
Goose Creek, SC 29445

Printed in the United States of America

ISBN: 979-8-9989246-1-3

For information on the content of this book,
email: shavettacraig42@gmail.com

Dedication

I would like to dedicate this book to my mother, Elizabeth Richardson, who is no longer with us, but through me, her spirit lives. I am picking up where you left off Momma. Thank you for all your love, support, and preparing me to be the woman that I am today. I pray that I am making you proud!!!

Elizabeth Richardson 12/11/1949-03/26/2006

Thank you to my "Pops" Graylin Richardson and Shirley Richardson for seeing my vision and believing in me to see it come to pass.

Table of Contents

Shavetta Craig

First Aid Kit

To be the one you come to,
And be a rescue.
To be the soothing to your scar,
And to bring out of you that person you truly are.
To be to your brokenness the cure,
And be a faithful and loyal friend for sure.
To be a protection like a band-aid,
And ensuring that my kindness and
thoughtfulness will never fade.
To be an antidote,
And inspire you with my words on a note.
To be an essential need,
And the healing to your bleed.
To be the listening ear to be your comfort,
While being a treatment with all efforts.
To be the CPR when you are out of breath,
And to love you until death.
To be the reasoning that on life and yourself you won't quit,
As I was created to be a first aid kit.

My Assignment

I was created for you,
To let you know that you are a virtue.
In God and me I need you to believe,
So to my words and actions cleave.
My image is a desire,
As it's for me to inspire.
Encouragement I'm supposed to give,
And giving you a reason to keep going and to live.
I'm that comfort to a need,
As my personality and character knows how
to bring a calmness and cease a bleed.
Supporting I know how to do so well,
So in my presence dwell.
To my light, shine, glow, brightness, and illuminating spirit grip,
As with gifts and talents I am equipped.
It's written and expressed so read it and grasp it and run,
Because it's for you, so I will be here until my work is done.
I have a power to reach and captivate,
As my hands were created to be great.
I cook to feed, give the best hugs, massage
to relieve stress, and poetry I write,
I am here for you to be a delight.
Love is all me,
And it's for me to show and display it to thee.
Favor and discernment to me is sent,
As I understand the details, instructions,
and purpose of my assignment.

I Will Be

The hug that you need,
That peels off the layers of your hurt, pain, brokenness, and bleed.
The spark to your day,
And your sunshine ray.
The change to your spirit,
And the purpose that you don't quit.
The reason that you smile again,
And being a good and meaningful friend.
The reflection of God that we love,
And the positive thoughts that you are thinking of.
The joy that you have,
And the fulfillment to the void in your
heart to make you again laugh.
The encouragement to my words spoken,
And that rare token.
The inspiration that you see,
As this person I will be.

He Stepped In

When I was defeated,
Mercy and grace came to complete it.
In my mind when the enemy tries to tap,
Wisdom and knowledge got in the gap.
Of my sins,
The blood wins.
When I was broken,
Love was the token.
When my flesh wanted to take control,
The spirit rise in my soul.
When trouble stir,
A way out occur.
When the situation went bleak,
A miracle peak.
When my back was against the wall,
My needs He met them all.
When I wanted to become a ghost,
His power and strength became my host.
When I didn't know what to do,
He showed up with my blessing in view.
When I was in a crunch,
His anointing poured down on me a bunch.
When I make mistakes,
He forgives and forgets and never forsakes.
No matter my situation or where I have been,
Jesus He stepped in.

It's In The Word

Let not your heart be troubled,
For your situation God will bless you with double.
For we walk by faith not by sight,
Jesus is my light.
Ask and it shall be given, seek and ye shall find,
knock and the door will open unto you,
In timing God will release your blessings and miracles do.
Trust in the Lord with all your heart,
From the will of God don't be apart.
Cast all your cares upon Him,
And He will see you thru the dim.
Pray without ceasing,
And you will see increasing.
I can do all things thru Christ that strengthens me,
And I won't give up I will do what God called me to be.
The Lord is my light and my salvation; whom shall I fear,
Because His presence is always near.
The Lord is my Shepherd; I shall not want,
Needs will be met and prayers answered with gaunt.
Now faith is the substance of things hoped for,
the evidence of things not seen,
And on His understanding I will lean.
Take heed to what you read and heard,
Because all you need it's in the word.

Trust God

Don't go by how it looks,
Faith is all it took.
Things may have been lost,
But it will be replenished and replaced with your belief cost.
Yes money is getting less,
Don't doubt because with your overflow you will be bless.
Don't get discouraged by the view,
Hold on to God, He has you.
We can get weak,
But let the Holy Spirit to you speak.
He won't leave you out on a limb,
Your blessings in His timing He will release them.
In your problems don't waddle or squirm,
In the will of God stand firm.
Now it may look like nothing,
But God will turn it into something.
You are frustrated, depressed, sad, angry, stressed,
and losing sleep because of no peace,
Rest in the Lord's presence and He will grant you an increase.
It's a lot to bear,
Just know you are not alone God is still there.
You get worried because a way out you can't see,
Don't give up on you or God a brighter future for you will be.
If you serve a Mighty God nod,
No matter how things look, seems, or go always trust God.

The Impossible

No more rainy days,
And seeing God work in many ways.
Things going always right,
God will remove the dark to bring light.
Not judging from envy or strife,
But God is the answer to take over your life.
Being stubborn to the core,
Until the Holy Spirit on you pour.
Will break the spell,
And send it back to hell.
The curse will be cast,
And will remain in the past.
The tears try to destroy,
But our God will deliver joy.
Temptation makes you weak,
But change and deliverance will take charge and you seek.
The gloomy cloud that follows,
But the sun will shine brighter tomorrow.
To having nothing,
And then an overflow of something.
You continue to see less,
But the unexpected turnaround has you now bless.
Our God is unstoppable,
And He can do the impossible.

In God

We trust,
And doing His will and ways are a must.
Put Him first,
And for His living water thirst.
Know that He is real,
And He has the power to deliver, set free, and heal.
We can have life,
And overcome our strife.
We will have light,
And gain sight.
Faith we will build,
And by He is spirit be fulfilled.
His love receive,
And in Him believe.
Cast all your cares,
And His goodness He wants us to share.
He is our strength and rod,
Everything we need is in God.

He Laid Down His Life

We are free,
Because of what Jesus did for thee.
We could never repay the price,
For our sins He did the ultimate sacrifice.
Worthy are none of us,
That's why we owe it all to Jesus.
We owe Him all the honor and praise,
He resurrected in three days.
Stand tall and stretch your arms wide,
To symbolize the cross on which Jesus died.
Victory is ours today,
Because Jesus made a way.
We can get pass the strife,
We have life because He laid down His life.

Nothing But The Blood

It's my protection every day,
And I pled it when I pray.
It kept me,
And from it the enemy flee.
That can cleanse my sins,
And thru me it's within.
It's my safety net,
To take control of me I will let.
It's no stranger,
It protects me from harm and danger.
It makes me pure,
And guides me for sure.
It gets me thru my battles,
And it sets me free as the enemy spa dado.
That makes me whole,
And creates a new image in my soul.
It washes away like a flood,
Nothing but the blood.

Hold On

God has your hand,
By your right side He stands.
You will see the results,
And waiting and patience will not be an insult.
He will see you thru the quest,
And then He will grant you rest.
The unseen will be shown clear,
Just don't fear.
Faith takes you thru the process,
So you can be bless.
Everything may appear and look bleak,
Just stay strong and don't become weak.
When it's just a little to grasp to,
Don't give in God got you.
Give Him all your might,
And He will reveal to you the light.
Continue to pray,
And watch God move in a mighty way.
You can't let the situation get the best of you,
Know who you are and know who you
serve and to God's word stay true.
You will make it from the doubts, brokenness, hurt,
disappointments, mistakes, burdens, and scorn,
Just remain faithful and hold on.

God You Are Hearing

God said listen to His voice,
But you want to do your choice.
God's way is correct,
But you want to follow your own intellect.
You need to take heed to what God say,
But you are disobedient and doing things your way.
Remember God is the Master,
Not you, for you are creating a disaster.
He is telling you what to do,
But you have a block up in your view.
You let pride, emotions, feelings, and
stubbornness get in your way,
Cast it away and in the will of God stay.
In your own direction and timing you are steering,
Even though God you are hearing.

Shavetta Craig

Say A Prayer

No matter what you are going through,
God has you.
In the midnight hour,
He is on duty to devour.
When you don't see a way,
On your knees stay.
Others are counting on you,
Talk to God on their behalf too.
It's a conversation,
To see you thru your tribulations.
It's the answer to the solution,
To see past the pollution.
From pain to joy,
And yokes it destroys.
Seal it with an Amen,
And do it constantly as you can.
The best thing to do,
Is to say a prayer for you.

Don't Lose Sight

Of putting God first always,
Because of what He does for you He deserves all your praise.
On what you asked God for,
In His timing the blessing will be at your door.
On all you have done,
Stay patient they will see your heart and
love and know that you are the one.
On your dreams,
And having the right people on your team.
On those who are always there for you,
They will forever be in your corner and to you be true.
On the impossible,
Because God is able.
On a love that remains,
They will be there like a permanent marker stain.
Better doesn't mean that it is,
Stick with what and who you know because
fire can ignite again from a fizz.
On what you are going thru because you will get over this,
Whatever it is heal, mend, change, and dismiss.
It doesn't take much just a little,
Of faith, love, and hope to grew just keep God and
Jesus with you while you are in the middle.
Of the bigger picture,
It will take the good, bad, and the ugly in your life to be richer.
Continue to pray and do right,
And don't lose sight.

Teach Us To Pray

With our mouth will come a sound,
To say something profound.
With the tongue confess,
And this should become our daily assignment with progress.
It's to our Father that we speak,
As His will we seek.
Out loud, on our knees, or in a place secretly,
He will hear us as our bond with Him is the key.
Results will produce,
When a talk with Him we are introduced.
What we are going thru let us with Him share,
He already knows but He wants to see that we
have the time to get before Him and care.
He wants to see our hearts,
Submitting to Him is how it starts.
We have to have an open mind,
And guidance from Him find.
Establishing a relationship with Him is the concept,
As Him we accept.
Let our sins, mistakes, troubles, tribulations,
and storms be known,
But pray for others and not just our own.
Our Father it's your way,
So teach us to pray.

If Not Me Then Who

Can forgive your sins,
Cleanse you and pour my spirit within.
Will make a way,
And provide an answer when you pray.
Will dry your tears,
And take away your fears.
Will provide,
And lead you and guide.
Will die and sacrifice,
And pay the ultimate price.
Will keep you protected,
And heal, deliver, and set free when infected.
Will love you unconditionally,
And your purpose see.
When trials you face,
Will fill you with mercy and grace.
Can save your soul,
As the Holy Spirit take control.
Can let you see,
That I Am the great I Am for thee.
Can perform miracles and do the impossible in your life,
And see pass your strife.
Can show signs and wonders,
And is with you on earth and up yonder.
Can be your Potter and you the clay,
To mold you so you won't stray.
Who will never leave or forsake you,
If not me then who?

Gods Going To

Change, create a new image and prepare them for reconcile,
So that this time around you will stay
together and will always smile.
Take an imperfect you,
And display a new creature in you as a transformation He will do.
See you thru any storms, and perform miracles out of the norm.
See you out of darkness into light, He is going to do a reverse,
And use you as an example to break the generational curse.
Get what was crooked back aligned,
And He will do the impossible and wonders as a sign.
Show up and show out,
As He produces blessings that makes you praise and shout.
Give you that house to call home that you desire,
Because your faithfulness, gratefulness, thankfulness,
and humbleness He admires.
Answer your prayers,
Because you were patient and waited on Him, so in
His timing He will show how much He cares.
Grant you the abundance of unconditional love,
Because He is pleased with you and so for you,
He will go beyond and above.
Rebuke the lies,
And take away the disguise.
Give you peace, and anything not of Him He will release.
Provide your needs,
Because of your faith of a mustard seed.
If following and believing in Him you continue to do,
The unexpected and suddenly things God's going to.

Ask God

What to do,
And what's the plans He has for you.
To let you know what you are doing wrong,
And where you are weak to make you strong.
To help you with temptations and
distractions that comes your way,
And how to pray.
For knowledge, wisdom, and power,
And negative thoughts devour.
To take away fear,
And let faith and trust substitute there.
To give you peace,
And anything not of Him release.
To put away your pride,
And let communication, compromising, consistency
and committing be your guide.
To show you favor,
And not man but Him to be your Savior.
How to love show,
And how to let someone know.
For His protection,
And direction.
For joy and happiness,
And more of Him than less.
To be your armor and rod,
Whatever you need ask God.

Wait

For the timing that God will bless you,
Because patience is a virtue.
For the right career,
God has you so don't fear.
For your God given mate,
Hold on for you they will be great.
The journey has to take its course,
Faith, trusting, and praying are your resource.
The increase, overflow, and miracles will take place,
But there is a process you will have to face.
Staying for the long haul is your endurance,
And God's promises are your reassurance.
For in the position you need to be,
Being able to weather the storms, trials and
tribulations, and challenges God needs to see.
Blessings come at a price,
You too have to become a sacrifice.
Just like a fish to bait,
On God wait.

Bread Of Life

Gods power,
So of your sins they can be devoured.
Shedding of light,
So from darkness you can do right.
God's word to read,
And by it take heed.
His life He gave,
So confess and be saved.
Prayers to get you thru,
And having faith do.
Righteousness to your soul feed,
And know that Jesus is all you need.
Let love in your heart saturate,
As it heals and provides a clean slate.
Mercy and grace sustain,
To correct your mistakes and pain.
Fight thru your strife,
With the bread of life.

Let God Be God

Timing is the key,
It's going to take that if we are going to be.
We may not see it but God do,
When the reconciliation will take place between me and you.
It's not meant to be rushed or forced,
Let God and it will be on course.
It's going to take Him to make this right,
But on reconciling we shouldn't lose sight.
He can do the impossible,
For us being together again He will be responsible.
Don't take matters into your own hands,
Let God do it because for us He stands.
If we do it we will create a mess,
God will handle it so it can be bless.
It's no time to worry,
Give it to God and He will bring to the situation glory.
It's not for us to fix,
That's why God has to be in the mix.
For us to be it's going to take His mercy, grace, and rod,
So let Him do it let God be God.

And There Was Light

Problems continue to pile,
Keep your faith you will again smile.
The greatness in you is hidden,
So tell your flaws good riddance.
Darkness is all you see,
Tell light be.
So much is happening around you,
Hold on great things God will do.
Out you can't see,
God says believe in me.
Your situation is trying to keep you blind,
Continue to trust God His solution you will find.
Have faith and be brave,
The way for you God will pave.
Just don't lose sight,
Because God will show up and there was light.

Resuscitate

Lord we are at your mercy,
For a change we are thirsty.
Right now, we are in a comatose state,
Bring us back to a new life that your potter hands will create.
We have been this way too long,
In your will is where we will dwell and become strong.
It's time for surgery,
To repair, restructure, review, revise, and reset the injuries.
The mind will think great thoughts,
As wisdom, knowledge, awareness, and peace are brought.
The spirit is filled with all the fruits and great things,
As serenity and healing it brings.
As the soul rejuvenates the purpose it's to do,
This time it will follow thru.
As the heart is transformed to a new rhythm beat,
We are in alignment now as the new reflection is complete.
When we gasp for our first new breath of air,
We breathe and cough out the former and inhale the fresh
start of the goodness that's in the atmosphere there.
Our eyes will open to a new view,
Thank you, Lord, because we were touched and worked on by you.
We will hear the sound of glory,
As we are brought back to life with a new story.

We now speak life,
After being cut away from our strife.
Damage has been done,
But we were corrected by the Mighty One.
Reconstruction was necessary,
Because we were drowning, failing,
sinking, and contaminated very.
Timing it took,
As we have a new look.
God is pleased because the outcome is great,
Because us God had to resuscitate.

But God

When I want to go insane,
Humble you make me remain.
For the mistakes that I do,
You still always come thru.
When I'm at the end of the rope,
You show up with hope.
When problems and troubles on me rains,
Right on time blessings you give for me to gain.
When I say God, please, you bring comfort and an ease.
When I can't and don't see a way, you show up to save the day.
When I see nothing in the account,
Suddenly you raise the amount.
When so much floods my mind,
A release you send so peace I can find.
I can't do,
But unexpectedly the possible you put in my view.
When I struggle to see what I deserve,
So when I wait the promises start appearing from your reserve.
When my eyes can't see, Faith,
He presents to me.
When I have put my all to get to the top
but something knocks me down,
You pick me up and turn things around.
When I say I'm done,
You continue to remind me with words,
Oh ye of little faith trust in me the One.
When things get hard,
Here comes relief and I smile and laugh and say but God.

God

Will never leave or forsake,
And see pass your sins and mistakes.
Will always be by your side,
And will provide.
Will make a way for you to come through,
And regardless of what you did He will always have you.
Will never lie,
So on His word rely.
Will do what He promised He will do,
So have faith and hope as a brighter future you will view.
Who created you and knows your life's plan,
Please just count on Him and not man.
On time He will be,
So be still, pray, wait, and trust and your blessings you will see.
Is a protection like an amour, shield, and rod,
He will do it because I'm talking about our God.

Shavetta Craig

My God Is A Healer

I don't care what the doctor say,
Things changes when you pray.
No matter the condition,
Your life can transition.
You can be down today,
But deliverance is on the way.
Don't let the situation get you down,
God is getting your attention and turning things around.
It doesn't take much,
Be set free by God's touch.
Don't let the past finder you,
Learn from it, move on, and let your future be your view.
Your body will mend,
And you will have great health again.
Yes, the enemy is a stealer,
But my God is a healer.

The Impossible Possible

When I dig myself into a hole,
You create a tunnel for me to get out as a way maker is your role.
When it was never,
You prove them wrong every time because with
God we will have future endeavors.
When they say I don't want you or love you anymore,
A change of heart on them God pours.
With a small seed, you bless so many needs.
A child is birth from a barren womb,
And you raised Lazarus from his tomb.
Even when we don't deserve it you always make a way,
Miracles you perform every day.
When I fail,
You correct me to prevail.
When I see nothing,
Suddenly and unexpectedly, you bless me with something.
When I wasn't great, a new image you create.
You fed the multitude,
From little to an abundance of food.
When our faith is weak,
Oh ye of little faith I Am the I Am,
I got you He speaks.
Nothing is too hard for thee,
Trust in Him and you will see.
My God is so incredible,
Because He makes the impossible possible.

Thanking You In Advance

Things will be how you have planned for them to be,
By faith and trust we will see.
It is our time and season,
As thy faithfulness, patience, hope, and prayers are the reasons.
We truly have to believe,
So if we ask, seek, and knock we shall receive.
For greatness we are ready,
And we will walk the journey steady.
What was lost will be found,
As we have improved this time around.
It's time for the next step,
And the promises and purpose to be kept.
To dream and see it come true,
As it is done by you.
Even thru our mess, good and bad,
You will still favor us as you bless us
with the best life we ever had.
Our storms and challenges will turn into our victory,
As you get all the glory.
Winning for us I know,
Because very soon we will reap the increase,
enlarging of our territory and our overflow.

We may not see it now but it's our approach,
As faith is our coach.
We will see better days,
And to you we give praise.
Waiting will pay off good,
As opportunities, growth, elevation, and
blessings will happen as they should.
So for the businesses, careers, house, breakthroughs,
resources, love, togetherness, reuniting, finances, peace,
joy, happiness, endurance, security, move and romance,
God we are thanking you in advance.

The Angels

They praise and glorify God,
Holy, Holy, Holy as the rod.
Against evil they guard,
To reveal what's coming so things won't be hard.
They are here to protect,
Because they know that we are not perfect.
They are the chosen messengers,
To bring life and peace to all and keep us from danger.
Our guardian,
To deter us from sin.
To carry out God's plan,
And to be a ministering spirit to all man.
Miracles they too perform,
And the calmness during the storm.
To us they speak,
When we are weak,
They are a covering,
And to our soul they sing.
They communicate God's revelations,
And see thru His declarations.
They care for us at death,
As they comfort until our last breath.
They encourage us,
And deliver us from the wicked just like Jesus.
Our supernatural being,
And our faith of seeing.
They capture our spirit to keep it from hell,
So thankful for the angels.

The Names Of Jesus

The Prince of Peace,
A joy, grace, Love, hope and happiness He release.
King of Kings,
Delight of His glory He brings.
He is Alpha and Omega,
Our Counselor and Savior.
The Holy and Righteous One,
Our daily bread God gave His Son.
The Lamb of God,
Who is our Shepherd and our rod.
Our Bread of Life,
Who died for our sins and strife.
The Lord of Lords,
Who shields us with His sword.
A Teacher to teach,
And with ministry to reach.
The Great Messiah,
Who is our desire.
The Light of the World,
Who blesses every man, woman, boy and girl.
That Morning Star,
It shines bright even from a far.

He is The Way,
Who reveals, show up, performs miracles,
and do the impossible every day.
He is the Chief Cornerstone,
So we are never alone.
The Anointed One,
So His will be done.
He is The Truth,
And our fountain of youth.
On the throne as High Priest,
He is the beginning and the end to say the least.
Immanuel God with us,
Oh, wonderful the names of Jesus.

Thru Faults

In your own mess,
God will still bless.
When you fail,
God will show up and prevail.
When your mistakes pile,
God will forgive you and still smile.
As you continue to sin,
God still will give you the ability to win.
When you do things your way,
He blesses you to see another day.
As you scrape,
God makes a way an escape.
When you deceive,
God still makes it so you can receive.
From your wrong,
God continues to make you strong.
When you don't deserve,
God is still on time to serve.
God picks you back up and rewards you with good results,
For you thru faults.

Keep Your Focus On

Only God has and knows the plan,
So don't compete, worry about, or depend on man.
By others you will be let down,
But God is faithful and will always be around.
Let Him lead and don't fear,
As your life direction He steers.
Don't dwell on what man do or say,
Keep your faith and always pray.
To your destiny and how you will get there,
So perseverance, stride, willpower, and
determination carry it with you everywhere.
Your dreams ahead,
And mending from when you bled.
Moving forward,
And trusting the Lord as to your future you seek towards.
The progress and healing after the scorn,
On God keep your focus on.

Like A Mighty Wind

To see God manifest,
As we are about to be bless.
Hearts will mend,
As the struggles and the same will end.
For the troubles endured,
Miracles will happen for sure.
What was promised will pour down like a flood,
And it will be rewarding like the blood.
The storms will cease,
And bring to you peace.
The hinderance will blow away,
As we embark on a new day.
Your past will bring forth great fruits,
From that mustard seed planted to root.
New things in our lives will begin,
And it will come thru like a mighty wind.

Shall

Have miracles and blessings to receive,
So in God I must believe.
Be fruitful and multiply,
And on the prayers, wait and process rely.
See better days,
So in advance I will thank God and give Him praise.
Reap because I continue to have faith and trust,
Because not giving up, drawing weary, or fainting are a must.
Walk into what God has for me,
It's my time to manifest to my destiny.
Have the favor to win,
Because from here on out this is my season that I am in.
Reach higher heights,
As my future has gotten bright.
Give God all the honor, credit, and glory,
Because of Him I made it this far and I will share my story.
See God's will be done,
As His timing is always right, so I patiently wait on
Him because who else can do it, there is none.
God is my Father, best friend, provider, protector, and pal,
And He is my everything and for me He shall.

Confessing

That the impossible is happening for thee,
And what was asked, prayed for, and spoken we will see.
That love and encouragement we will share,
And our winning season I declare.
That the generational curse, addictions, and lacks are broken,
Because the best and better over us will happen that was spoken.
From yesterday we will not be the same,
And I'm claiming that in Jesus' name.
That faith and hope are seeing us through,
Because in due timing the reaping, receiving,
and revealing God will do.
Greatness and abundance all around,
And the manifest will be profound.
That God's favor He will show and prove,
So get ready for Him to move.
An increase over finances I decree,
And we shall be debt free.
Speaking over lives miracles and blessings,
For me and others this I'm confessing.

A Feast

Prepare for,
Because you are in the season of more.
The good for you to eat,
Even though you the enemy tried to defeat.
For the going through and hardships that wasn't pleasurable,
But because of your faith you are about
to receive the unmeasurable.
You persevered with the test, mess, and burdens sent,
As peace, joy, happiness, and love will be your enjoyment.
For an endurance,
And God with you is the reassurance.
It's to fulfill,
Because done will be God's will.
So you will never want again,
As blessings, increase, manifestation, and
overflow will become a trend.
You overcame all the things that came to you the beast,
Now the time has come as God has for you a feast.

Break It, Cut It, Kill It

You need to free yourself from the ties,
And speak and follow the truth not the lies.
It's trying to destroy you,
Help and guidance seek you do.
That thing or things that keeps causing a problem,
Find the right solution to solve them.
Get it at the root,
And those bad habits boot.
Don't allow it to come back,
No longer let this hinderance be your attack.
Let it go,
And to temptation say no.
Let what has a hold on you crumble,
No longer be stubborn but humble.
Your affliction let them die,
And to what is causing hurt and pain say goodbye.
Let it burn,
And a change yearn and your life turn.
Face it and conquer it every bit,
So your demon break it, cut it, kill it.

Dear God

First, I want to say Thank You,
I don't deserve it but for all you do.
For my sins and wrongs please forgive me,
Because what you have planned for me,
I must keep my faith to see.
I'm not perfect and at times I disobey,
But you love me regardless and still tell
me that things will be okay.
As my life can be a mess,
God me you still come through for and bless.
My struggles, storms, challenges, and trials keep me doubtful
that it taunts me to believe that your promises and rewards
for me that I won't reach them like they are too far,
But you always show me that on time God you are.
I know you hear my prayers and see when I cry,
But to trust in you I do even when it's hard I continue to try.
Sometimes it may not be strong but my
faith I will always hold to,
But God know that I love you.
I catch myself to complain, doubt, fear, worry and grumble,
But I have to remind myself to remain thankful,
grateful, faithful, and humble.

To see others have plenty and getting it easy and
having it the wrong way makes me furious,
But I still pray for them but why not me makes me curious.
I will continue to wait and do what's right,
Because my overflow, increase, and rise are on
the way and my future will be bright.
Let me continue to dwell in your glory and
be protected by your shield and rod,
And thank you for your mercy, grace, peace,
love, and kindness dear God.

Shavetta Craig

God It's All You

To wake me up every day,
And always providing a way.
To make sure that I never quit,
Because in your timing my blessings are going to hit.
My prayers answered to see,
Because I can't make it without thee.
To give me the hope and future that I need,
Because your love, mercy, grace, favor, miracles
and the impossible are how you feed.
To help me to see the better,
As my storms I weather.
For faith for me to view,
God, I love you.
For your will and plan,
And to know that I can.
The timing that is just right,
And providing me with light.
The blessings that I receive,
Because in you I trust and believe.
To make me wait,
Because you want me to learn patience for what is great.
The victory, overflow, and increase,
And giving me peace.
Creating me,
As a reflection of you I want to be.
Everything for me that you do,
God it's all you.

Praying

A prayer for you I say out loud and whisper,
In God's timing we will wait for a change to occur.
What we ask God can do,
Healing I spoke over you.
I say a prayer every day,
I wait patiently for God to make a way.
His will be done,
So it's up to the Father and the Son.
Prayer is a part of daily life,
To heal, deliver, and set free our strife.
Prayers is my all,
As the name of Jesus,
I call.
To pray is all I was taught and know,
With faith the answer will show.
In God's will be staying,
As for you I'm praying.

God Why Me

When things bad seems to happen, this is the question we ask,
But trusting God is the task.
God doesn't want to punish you,
But going thru is the virtue.
From God things you will have to earn,
And from pain, hurt, suffering, delays, mistakes,
storms, and challenges are how you will learn.
God won't put too much on you than you can bare is true,
If He put it on you then He will see you thru.
Things may seem odd,
But never lose your faith in God.
He knows that you can carry the load,
You are equipped for this so be a reflection
of God and do what He has told.
Why not you,
What Jesus did for you a sacrifice for Him you can't do?
Easy is not the way,
You are going to go thru to get for what you pray.
You must put some hard work in,
Then you can win.
God wants to see your heart,
And being able to sustain the battles, what's being thrown at
you, what's unfair and all the obstacles are how you start.
From trials and tribulations there is a great,
So the end results anticipate.
When the finished product, rewards, and the victory you will see,
Then you won't question God why me.

I Trust You

With my life choices,
And hear only you God and not listen to others voices.
With the words that you say,
And the plan you have for me that's coming my way.
With the storms I go thru,
I still look to you.
With my life plan, You know and created it not man.
Thru the wait and process,
My patience is how I will be bless.
When I don't see,
You always whisper God, I got thee.
Even when doubt and fear ponder,
I just can't let my faith wonder.
Waiting on you I will do,
Because God,
I trust you.

Shavetta Craig

Only You

Can make a way,
And guides, provides, and protects me every day.
Have the master plan,
Who I trust and not man.
Let me see tomorrow,
And bring joy from sorrow.
Can understand and see my pain,
And grant me favor to sustain.
Can bless me,
And glory see.
Can give me healing,
And peace feeling.
With my day start,
And you have my heart.
The impossible do,
God only you.

Choose

God first,
And with Him you will never hunger or thirst.
Listen to what He say,
And in His timing, He will answer to what you pray.
Then put you next,
Don't let anyone make your life complex.
Go with God's plan,
So enjoy your life and make no sacrifices for
any undeserving woman or man.
To have peace,
Your burdens and doubts please release.
To love who will truly love you unconditionally back,
And willing to serve a purpose in your life and
provide whatever is needed to avoid a lack.
The happiness that is given,
It's the true meaning and reason for living.
Your insanity,
So sleep at night and follow your destiny.
To live,
And do as God does and that's give.
Step out on faith you will have nothing to lose,
What's right for you choose.

It's Knocking At Your Door

The blessings that await,
And the opportunities that are going to make your life great.
The manifest on the horizon,
And your season to win.
The overflow and increase,
And the needed peace.
The joy to endure,
And happiness for sure.
Your success, breakthrough, turn around,
comeback, and for you to soar,
And it's there too your elevation and so much more.
The answer to your prayers,
And the one for you who cares.
Love that wants to captivate you,
And this time it will sustain, fulfill, and stay true.
Potentials to see,
And a dream becoming a reality.
Your future,
And the Holy Spirit revealing to you the bigger picture.
The best and the good,
And everything happening as it should.
God so in your life He will continue to pour,
What's been chasing you it's knocking at your door.

That's What Makes God Proud

When we give Him our all,
And on His name call.
When in Him we trust,
And know following His will is a must.
When in faith we walk,
And to Him we talk.
When we don't look at the situation but believe in the results,
And we continue to persevere through the insults.
When we can go through and know that we are going to make it,
And we don't draw weary, faint, or quit.
When we cast upon Him our burdens and cares,
And daily say our prayers.
That we can be hurt but mend,
And know if He did it before He can do it again.
That we know that things are going to get better,
And any problems, setbacks, and dilemmas we can weather.
Even through the trials, tribulations, challenges,
storms, and sufferings we continue to give Him
glory, honor, and praise shout loud,
These are the things that what makes God proud.

You Are Not Done With Us Yet

Blessings are on the rise,
And it will be unexpectedly, suddenly, and by surprise.
God is just getting started,
He is here to restore the broken hearted.
The impossible and miracles will take place,
So know that anything that comes for you,
know you will be able to face.
The overflow and increase are coming for thee,
Just watch and see.
You are approaching the manifest,
So let your mind, soul, and spirit be at rest.
The best to come takes time,
So walk by faith when the challenges chime.
When we ask, seek, and knock,
What's for us will not be blocked.
This is just the beginning,
This is the season and year for winning.
On your timing let us wait and not regret,
Because God, you are not done with us yet.

When It's Right

It will happen for you,
So praying continue to do.
Things will fall into line,
Regardless of what you are going through you will be fine.
Life will get better,
Just continue to be a go getter.
You will get the reward for your labor,
Because it's on your life to have favor.
You will know,
And no one will be able to stop your overflow.
What's for you, be ready to receive,
Just have faith, hope, patience, and you must trust and believe.
It will shock you and blow your mind,
Because the best is after you to find.
Timing will be on your side,
And whatever you prayed and asked for God will provide.
In you God will delight,
When it's right.

I Will Trust In The Lord

When I get weak,
The Lord's will, I will seek.
I have to give it to Him,
He's my light when I'm dim.
When I need to get a prayer thru,
He is my breakthrough, Lord, I love you.
From what I can't see,
I will declare the victory.
Thru my strife,
He has my life.
With everything that is within me,
It belongs to thee.
When I shout,
He is my way out.
With all my wit,
I will serve Him every bit.
Faith is my source,
And He is my course.
In Him I believe,
As His love I receive.
You will always be my reward.
So I will trust in the Lord.

The Four C's- In God

Communication
You must talk with God every day. And that's with prayer.
Let God know how much you love Him, trust Him, obey Him,
and need Him. Also, by telling others about Him. God is always
listening so speak to Him. He wants to hear from you.

Commitment
Always put God first. Read your Bible and stay spiritually
feed. Doing what's right. Serving Him. His way and
will are the only way. So give your life to Him.

Compromise
God awaits you so meet Him half way. It is not about you it's
about helping others and showing them the way. There is 24 hours
in a day God doesn't require much of our time just make sure you
give Him your heart and attention at some point in the day.

Consistent
Don't stop praying, serving, doing, and giving. Continue to give
your time, talent, and tithes. Continue to improve. We can ask
for forgiveness and repent as needed because we are not perfect.
Continue to love, be kind, helpful and patient. Continue to grow.

Satan Get Behind Me

You try to catch me when I'm weak,
Just like a snake on me you sneak.
You try to make me lose sleep,
As on me and in my mind you creep.
You get on my nerves,
But a Mighty God I serve.
You never want to see anything go right,
So stay in the dark because I'm going to the light.
All you are is the destruction and pollution,
Thank God for common sense because I
seek God for all my solutions.
You always causing a problem,
But I have God, He always solve them.
You really want control,
But guess what you won't because God has my soul.
Yes, I make mistakes, sin, fall and slip,
But repentance and forgiveness are the
key so I just gave you a free tip.
You always try to get in my way,
But it's going to stop today.
I'm going to stay and remain strong,
So don't get me to do wrong.
You meddle too much,
But me you can't touch.
With and for God I will always be,
So Satan get behind me.

Created

With the sweat and tears,
And got stronger from the fears.
From the pain endured,
Faith, strength, determination, and willpower I'm cured.
Still here from the battles fought,
From the mistakes lessons were taught.
Survived the hurt given,
Forgiveness is why I'm living.
To sustain thru the lacks,
And from the storms bounce back.
To carry the heavy load,
And to make it down the rugged road.
To pick up the pieces again,
And knows what it takes to make love mend.
To get out of a jam,
My scars are who I am.
For when things get rough,
And knows when enough is enough.
From falls again stand,
Because I have a purpose on this land.
That the sorrow, disappointment, and weakness were peeled,
As from brokenness I healed.
To handle the contractions,
White pressing thru the distractions.
The bad and ugly wasn't anticipated,
But thru it all I was created.

Continue To

When you fall,
Get back and up give it your all.
When you stumble,
Dust yourself off and remain humble.
When you are under an attack,
Trust God because He will give it all back.
When you fail,
Success is on the way for you to prevail.
When you don't see a way,
Continue to believe and pray.
When you are hurt and scorn,
Forgive and get the strength to move on.
When you are a mess,
This is when God does His best work because you, He will bless.
When you are about to lose your mind,
Just know peace you will find.
When someone leaves,
Know that God has someone better for you to cleave.
Everything happens for a reason,
Embrace the change, lesson, and rewards in that season.
Believe that you can,
And know everything works better with God's plan.
To love and better you,
And persevere continue to.

Standing In The Need Of Prayer

It's what we count on,
When we are scorn.
We face so many challenges and wrongs,
It's that power of prayer that keeps us strong.
It's needed every day,
For each other we must pray.
Life is tough,
And one prayer is not enough.
The pain needs to lift,
And this situation needs to shift.
It takes two or more to touch and agree,
To see a change or bring comfort to thee.
It can be silent or loud,
So it can be heard thru the clouds.
What we feel needs to dissolve,
But it will when prayer is involved.
It's the only thing to try,
For prayers we cry.
It's that needed solution,
To clear away our pollutions.
It keeps us calm,
When there is harm.
It keeps you sane,
From the hurt and pain.
We just need to know that you are there,
As we are standing in the need of prayer.

Like The Rainbow

It's bright,
And sheds light.
It creates a grin,
Many colors within.
It has two ends,
And it bends.
It shows thru the sun and rain,
And soothes thru the pain.
It appears and fade,
And is beautifully made.
It paints a marvelous scene,
And of it you become keen.
A smile that makes the heart glow,
Just like the rainbow.

Perfect

I know we won't be,
It's about me loving you and you loving me.
The storms will make us strong,
And ensure that our love will last long.
It's not being a saint,
It's the lifetime we will paint.
It's about not quitting but seeing the love thru,
You have flaws and I have mine too.
There will be good and bad days,
And getting thru challenges in so many ways.
We won't always see eye to eye,
But we will never tell our love goodbye.
Thru the sun and rain,
Respect, admiration, patience, growth, humbleness
and thankfulness we will gain.
When giving your all there's nothing to reject,
But for each other we are perfect.

Cast Away

The worry in your mind,
And peace find.
Things that are being a leach,
And a new direction reach.
The lust,
And believing God is a must.
The lies you tell,
And get back up from the times you fell.
The wicked ways,
Come to Jesus and give him praise.
Negative thoughts,
And then happiness to you will be brought.
The old,
And the greatness and better ahead behold.
The ungodly spirits,
And the righteousness dwell in it.
Every day I pray,
For these destruction to cast away.

Sustain

It keeps me equipped,
And floating and sailing as a ship.
It makes a mark,
So something amazing in you can spark.
It's the willpower to go,
It's the breath of God on you that He blows.
It makes you strong,
And stays long.
It never stops,
As mercy and grace on you it drops.
In you it's planted,
And gives access granted.
It that comfort shield,
And to it everything must yield.
It's simple and will remain,
The glory you sustain.

Proof

Evidence of things not seen,
And with faith become keen.
A sign or prophetic word as confirmation,
Declaring, receiving, claiming, and decreeing are explanations.
The impossible being done,
Miracles happening one by one.
Making a way,
It's always on time with no delay.
He did it before,
And again He is doing it, blessings at your door.
You inhale and exhale,
And with having nothing He provides and prevail.
You are alive and over your head is a roof,
Mercy and grace are your living proof.

Peace

Free your mind,
And relaxing thoughts find.
Always remain calm,
Because your burdens are with God in His palm.
Keep in your quite place,
And let silence be your case.
It's to refresh you,
And provide something new.
It's that thing we all need,
And with it our inner man we feed.
It puts you at ease,
So unwind, kick back, and release please.
It's a positive healing,
That gives you a great feeling.
It's the answer for every day,
And it's the inspiring way.
It soothes your soul,
And it dismisses the things in your life that takes toll.
So let destruction, chaos, and turmoil from your life cease,
And just live in peace.

Listen

To what is being said,
Meditate on it and in the right direction be led.
Very clearly,
And be very sincerely.
Not with your mouth but with your ear,
Carefully be attentive to what you hear.
To what God speaks,
His way and wisdom seek.
For the right voice,
And make a wisely choice.
And receive from the heart,
Comprehending and adhering the message is the art.
Is an action,
That requires no distraction.
It's a thinking process,
That can result to success.
Advise, wisdom, knowledge, understanding,
help, or encouragement words spoken,
To take heed to what is said is a valuable token.
It can make your life glisten,
If you just listen.

Now

Is the time to see,
That better is waiting on thee.
Let knowledge, wisdom, and common sense click,
And to God's will and way stick.
Look from the dark to the light,
Your practices, failures, mistakes, and stumbles
should get you on the path to do right.
Put fear away as you have mercy and grace,
Because it's time to get in your rightful place.
Let your faith steer,
Because your breakthrough and blessing are near.
In God believe,
So a healing you can receive.
Give God your heart,
By letting Him take control is how it starts.
It's time to smile than frown,
And change must take place now.

Shavetta Craig

Day By Day

Let God be your resource,
And waiting and trusting on Him to keep you on course.
Let your spirit speak,
The flesh don't seek.
Take steps forward,
And better look towards.
Ask the Holy Spirit to lead you,
And be humble, thankful, and grateful for
everything for you that God will do.
Is a healing process,
Just know that you are bless.
Do something for someone else that is kind,
And keep a positive frame of mind.
Love more,
Give of yourself and bring peace, joy, and happiness galore.
Let victory be in your sight,
In timing your prayers will be answered just
keep and look towards the light.
Better days embrace,
Because you are making it on God's mercy and grace.
The only things to do is to have faith and pray,
And do this day by day.

Believe

In you,
And with God there's nothing impossible that you can't do.
That things will get better,
The challenges, tribulations, and storms weather.
That you serve a Mighty God,
And He is your protector shield and rod.
That your answered prayers are on the way,
And that you will have a happy life every day.
That you will elevate,
And greatness create.
That you will win,
No matter where you have been.
In what you speak,
And faith seek.
That you are a conqueror,
Because you were formed in the image of your Creator.
In your spirit man,
And you always can.
That you will make it through,
It all starts with the confidence in you.
That you will be on top,
Being consistent, progressing, praying,
hoping, and excelling don't stop.
For you to receive,
You must believe.

Reset

Even if you fail,
Again in the right direction you can sail.
Restore what was broken,
Repenting and forgiving from your lips should be spoken.
Revive your life,
So you have to be delivered from your strife.
Rebuild to make it sustain,
Faithful to God's destiny for you remain.
A do over do,
Repair what was despaired first start with you.
Moving forward means no looking back,
Let God led and stay on track.
Redirect your attention,
And release yourself from the tension.
Another chance you will get,
Don't rewind or reverse just hit reset.

Sometimes You Need To Be Uncomfortable

Things won't always go right,
God will shake you up to shed on you light.
You God has to break,
So you can understand the mistake.
What you did you have to feel,
And what you already have is for real.
The storms are to teach you,
Believe and a change do.
What was done will make you reflect, forgive, repent,
and restore because no one's perfect.
You have to experience the truth,
And grow up from your youth.
You need to get in your rightful place,
But know challenges you will face.
To get you on track God has to do the inedible,
So sometimes you need to be uncomfortable.

Shavetta Craig

Clothed Me

With your blood I'm covered,
And around me the angels hovered.
With the righteous way,
And in this vessel permanently stay.
Equip me for the battle,
And follow and be my reflection my shadow.
Anoint me with your oil,
And bring to me new soil.
With goodness, mercy and grace,
As your presence I embrace.
With the shield and rod,
I can never do it alone without you God.
With your favor,
And you lead me my Savior.
With a spirit of thanksgiving,
As humble and grateful I'm living.
Lord I need your spirit all over thee,
So I require you to clothed me.

Turn

Fears into faith,
For I will never leave nor forsake you the Lord saith.
Doubt into determination,
And fulfilling your destiny your declaration.
Worries into wonders,
And on God ponder.
Pollution into positivity,
Living and doing right will give you longevity.
Lust into love,
Stay focus, commit, and go beyond and above.
Hate into humble,
And let negativity crumble.
Burdens into blessings,
Give it to God and stop stressing.
Darkness into light,
And know that whatever you face or go thru,
you not giving up is your insight.
Failures into forgiveness,
And always try, do more and not less.
Bitter into better,
And be a go getter.
Problems into peace,
And things out of your control release.
Grief into grace,
And let mercy in to embrace.
Improvements always yearn,
And your wrongs into a right turn.

Shavetta Craig

Forgiven

For all the sins you have done,
And making God your number one.
For the pain cause,
And looking ahead and not back at the was.
For the lies told,
As now the truth you unfold.
For your mistakes,
And the hearts you break.
The bad and sad,
And now fulfilling your life with love and
laughter, things to make you glad.
For the wrongful repeats,
And knowing that repenting and changing
will make you complete.
For life's hardships and broken dreams,
But now being faithful on my team.
For the flaws in you, and the unfortunate things you do,
as you turn it around to become a virtue.
Do right while you are living,
For your old it has been forgiven.

Without A Trace

His spirit lives,
As His love He gives.
Just like air you can't see it but you can feel,
And by His stripes and power you are heal.
Many days we don't know how,
He is on time and works it out every time wow.
His presence is real,
As His blessings He reveals.
It's all about the unseen,
As on and by faith you lean.
He is with you,
As His mercy and grace carries you and is true.
Always forgive and repent,
His word, commandments and the righteous
path is a symbol of His prints.
When you are weak, He gives you the strength to become strong,
And so, you can do right from wrong.
When storms, conspiracies, and troubles brew,
The Savior, All Mighty One, Awesome, King of Kings, Lord of
Lords He will cease it, in still peace and fight the battle for you.
Alone you are not,
The all-powerful you He got.
Trust embrace,
As all these things He does without a trace.

Wait For It

It may seem long,
Continue to pray and keep your faith strong.
Though it tarry,
Trust God because your blessings and promises He carries.
Just because you ask for it, don't look for it to happen quick,
It will be given unto you, if in your trust in God you stick.
It's not that far away,
Be patient it will reveal any day.
Your day of victory is near,
And change, slowness, waiting and a pause don't fear.
A progress you will go thru,
And then in God's timing He will reward you.
And don't see it as God forgotten,
He knows when to do and what He has for
you is for you there is no stopping.
Greater things happen when it works like a snail,
Because it will take place unexpectedly
and suddenly so you can prevail.
It may take a while,
Continue to move forward and smile.
It won't just be handed to you,
So work, trust, and progress you will have to do.
What you yearn, you must earn.
The longer you wait, The bigger it will be great.
Learn to anticipate, be still and with what you
desire, deserve, and believe in don't quit,
Because favor, love, joy, happiness, endurance, financially
breakthroughs, careers and togetherness will come, wait for it.

Rise

From the sins that can cause you to be dead,
And the lies that you fed.
From the fears that consumes you,
And the deceitful things that you do.
From the misery, envy, jealousy and strife
in which you keep laying,
And only when you are in trouble you are praying.
From that demon you can't seem to defeat,
And the evil that keeps you running on your feet.
From the hurt, pain, brokenness and past you continue to carry,
And the addictions and habits to whom you marry.
From the negative thoughts,
And the shame and blame you brought.
From the bitterness you hold,
And the secrets you won't unfold.
From the image that you betray,
And not knowing how you are going to make it each day.
From your falls,
And not giving God your all.
From the blood on your hands,
And from the unrighteousness for which you stand.
From your guilt,
And the destruction you built.
In your life there can be a resurrection,
From choosing the wrong directions.
The signs and wonders happening around
you doesn't come by surprise,
Jesus is coming back, so from your unrighteousness rise.

The Signs

The storms that continue,
It's trying to stir you up to bring forth something new.
The chaos all around,
To shake you to make the right decisions to stay
with God so you can be solid and profound.
The dreams and sleepless nights,
It's time to love, live and do right.
The corrections, going back to true love, changing for the
better, staying true, and righteousness you avoid,
God is displeased and annoyed.
You keep seeking darkness instead of light,
The path to go, choices to choose and the
voice to listen to you lose sight.
You know what is right to do but you won't,
God's trying to get your attention, so His way do instead of don't.
You battle with which way to go,
As fear, hesitation, doubt, and misery consumes you so.
You are under attack,
Who will you surrender to so you can get back on track.
Your life is in a disarray,
For guidance pray.
The answer is right in front of you,
Step out on faith and do what you supposed to do.
No longer be blind and get align,
As God is revealing to you the signs.

Savor

Each day as it's your last,
And dwell on the present and future and not the past.
The laughter given,
And the purpose for living.
Love that is from the heart,
And from the smile you can't depart.
The eyes that shines,
And the thank you that makes things fine.
The happiness that makes you glow,
And all the great people that you know.
The thought that is on your mind,
And how someone to you has been kind.
That breath that you take,
And be proud of the progress you make.
That hug,
And that special person on who hand you tug.
To dream, to make memories and to create
something great is favor,
So live life and each moment savor.

Passion

To long for,
And a desire for more.
Something to learn,
And the ability to yearn.
To seek after,
And to bring comfort and laughter.
It's a drive,
With a feeling that brings you alive.
It's an endurance to be,
And purpose to see.
It's how forever is made,
And sustains not to fade.
That feel good,
And so affectionate as it should.
It's a sentiment reaction,
The emotion of passion.

Even When

Disasters we had to face,
And bitterness and unhappiness filled our space.
There wasn't a good life,
And we had to battle with,
Fight and couldn't control the strife.
There was always a fall,
So many times, on the name of Jesus I call.
It was so impossible to forgive,
I did it with healing and learned how to live.
Over and over again the same things kept happening,
It was a war because the enemy, temptations,
addictions, people, lies, deceit, and habits kept
intruding, harassing, being bold, taking control and
won't take no for an answer until it kept tapping.
Doubt took the best of us,
As we got anger, defensive and all you knew to do was fuss.
Hurt became a common thing,
As brokenness and tears it always brings.
Sorry you didn't say,
For a change I continue to pray.
Pain chimes,
And we had nothing, not even a dime.

There was no direction to go,
And a way out we couldn't find and all we heard was no.
There was fear and stubbornness,
The past had to go and we had to move on so
this time we could produce success.
All failed,
Just trust God He made things again to prevail.
You held back,
Your heart and mind were steering you on the right track.
We couldn't see it,
It took time for us to understand not to quit.
There were breaking points,
God took His time with us over many years
to anoint and get us yoked to joint.
You finally get yourself in order to correct and better
things from the shatters and the old you back then,
I will still love you even when.

Just Wait And See

For the faithfulness and labor,
My God had granted me favor.
Trusting I did but it was a challenge,
By faith I managed.
I was down, build up and had some hiccups again,
But know that bouncing back is the best way to mend.
I'm going to win,
Watch as I'm an example of victory as now it starts to begin.
It may have took a long while,
God's timing is everything to bring me a permanent smile.
What I asked and prayed for,
God will answer and provide more.
Rough things have been,
But God's will I'm in.
I was talked about, judged, lied on, and looked at funny,
But my testimony will prove how great my
God is as it's worth more than money.
The new image that will unfold,
And the blessings told.
As my failures and mistakes will bring forth my success,
And my humbleness, perseverance, thankfulness,
and gratefulness will make me bless.
The hinderance, burdens, doubts, and fears I surrender all,
And I will stand again from my falls.
New and improve,
As my God moves.
How God will bless me and anyone attached to me,
Just wait and see.

I'm Expecting

A great reward,
And a better future to seek towards.
A promising God's plan,
And to progress myself as an improving woman or man.
Greatness everlasting,
And joy, Love, peace, happiness, serenity, and security casting.
Hope to arise,
And blessings catching me by surprise.
For goodness to find me,
And my winning season see.
For the years to come to be kind,
With a purpose and fulfillment to find.
For God to do it,
And I won't quit.
For faith to show evidence,
As it leads the way with confidence.
So now the plan and thought I will see without rejecting,
Because what God had for me, I'm expecting.

Forgive And Forget The Past

What was done is a constant replay in your mind,
Peace you must find.
Don't let it eat you alive,
You got thru this anything you can survive.
What took place hurt but it didn't ruin you,
You are still here and staying strong you learned how to do.
You have a dream,
Get it done and let out all that frustration and steam.
It hurts like hell,
But get back up from where you fell.
Again believe,
And this time around greatness you will receive.
Don't let your history hinder you,
Just discover the amazing and incredible things for you to do.
They did and you did,
So of the malice, anger and bitterness get rid.
Once you have gotten pass it let it go,
And don't remember it and with the new flow.
Healing is the process,
So over what was done no longer stress.
Let your history spark your future with a blast,
As you forgive and forget the past.

A Time To Heal

For so long this world has been thru a lot,
God, faith, hope, and love are all we got.
We are supposed to live, move, and have our being,
For a while that's not what we were seeing.
The blood of Jesus was shed for all of our sins,
But others blood poured out from them
because of the color of their skin.
Unity, helping and coming together went out the door,
And giving more to the rich and forgetting the
middle class, low income, and the poor.
Promises were broken that was told,
As racism, hate, anger and injustice unfold.
It's not about who or what we believe in or the color of our skin,
It's about the love, kindness, care and
making a difference that is within.
With our actions Jesus is not pleased,
He is the way maker to show us how to get thru storms,
trials and tribulations and challenges to create ease.
We have to matter,
With all the shatter.
Having and living in peace is the way,
We need to continually pray.
We need to stop smiling in faces and then
stabbing others in the back,
We are better than this because wisdom, understanding,
thoughtfulness, consideration, trusting and believing we lack.

We have to repair this broken nation,
And make mending, a fresh start, a reset,
and a newness our declaration.
We must be able to breathe again,
And that on freedom and justice we will depend.
Regardless of your belief,
This nation deserves and needs a relief.
Bad and wrongdoings is not what this world is made of,
Because God is and we should be love.
Perfect this world will never be,
But greatness, better, improvements,
fairness and change we should see.
From our failures we should learn to bring forth success,
And it is for everyone to be bless.
Some may be happy and some may be sad,
But we can't continue on with what we had.
Justice is for all,
Even as we rise and when we fall.
This world is to be great,
So let's correct the mistakes.
We need to fade the fragments of despair,
And that for this nation we care.
God is who we should serve and He is
in control and has all power,
So do what's right and let the negativity devour.
Thru the hurt and pain that we feel,
Now is a time to heal.

Every Praise

For life,
And forgiving me of my sins and strife.
For making a way,
And in my right mind I stay.
Trusting you,
And letting victory be my view.
For answered prayers,
As your grace and mercy shows that you care.
When I can't see,
He always goes before me.
I lift my hands high,
As on His goodness I rely.
He has been too good to me,
As His love is the key.
I put my past to rest,
Because in me He sees my best.
Thank you, Lord and hallelujah I will say loud with my voice,
God gives me a reason every day to rejoice.
My praise I will give for all of my days,
Because due to God is every praise.

Rewrite

To a new chapter I need to go,
No rush take things slow.
Errors and mistakes I will correct,
Show improvement and change while
understanding that I'm not perfect.
A do over I will do,
And know that love can be true.
Things I will illuminate,
As a new me I will create.
This time it will have a happy ending,
As I have learned from my past and a
lifetime be will be spending.
Putting the wrong and negative to rest,
And from this moment on giving my very best.
Things I will erase,
And find myself in a better place.
Starting over is never a bad thing,
A turn around and shift is good and positive results bring.
Doing things right,
As I do in my life a rewrite.

Resilience

You it tried to defeat,
But you got back up on your feet.
It may have taken long,
But you remained strong.
Just like a ball you continued to bounce,
You didn't give up not one ounce.
With sweat and tears,
You overcame your fears.
You wouldn't stop until you win,
Only if they knew where you have been.
You had a rocky start,
But you gave it your all your heart.
You didn't look back,
Even while you were being attack.
You got weary and weak,
But your faith rise and peak.
You showed them what you are made of,
You got there by patience, humbleness, determination, and love.
Your faithfulness became your brilliance,
As you saw resilience.

Patience

Something to endure,
For peace, rewards and a sound mind are the cure.
With some it's long and others short,
So for what you want don't abort.
It's truly a virtue,
It's how God blesses you.
It's a process so wait,
What's the rush the timing will be great.
It's something to learn,
As strength and willpower, you will earn.
It will not happen right away,
Because you have to build trust and faith and always pray.
Don't focus on the challenges to get to where you are going,
Your perseverance keep showing.
It may seem like forever,
The storm weather.
The timing may seem ancient,
Because great things will happen for your patience.

Defeated

The bad habits that are taking over our souls,
And our flesh that wants to have control.
The multiple mistakes,
And the unwanted heartaches.
The hurt and pain that we feel,
And the temptations that don't want us to heal.
The enemy's plan,
And they can't that should be can.
The past that we should have left behind,
And the poison that consumes our mind.
In the sins that we dwell,
That's heading us to hell.
The negativity that holds us hostage,
As our lives it tries to demolish from not turning the page.
The fear that we live in,
And not seeing a smile or grin.
What's keeping us from our victory must be deleted,
As the unwanted thoughts, feelings, addictions,
habits, and doubts will be defeated.

Power

We hold,
And we stand tall and bold.
It's been in us all along,
We came together as we became strong.
In volumes we showed our strength,
As to see change, love, freedom, and unity at all lengths.
It was asked,
And we delivered on their task.
It spoke,
And we are woke.
Mighty are we,
And the best we will see.
We made the choice,
And they heard our voice.
We made history again,
And in God we trust as we mend.
A village it took,
As our nation we shook.
What came against us and tried to take us out we devour,
Because we have power.

Built

Dreams and goals you must accomplish,
And your journey finish.
Let your fear make you strong,
As faith and determination see you along.
Don't doubt what you can do,
Because I believe in you.
To create a desire into a reality,
And do it with all your abilities.
To reach higher heights,
And focus on it day and night.
To be amazing,
As your achievements we will be praising.
To conquer whatever comes your way,
As you soar each day.
To make a difference and stand tall,
Proud of you as you name of honor they call.
To shine,
You got this you will do and be fine.
To be a friend,
And when you fail just try again.
To climb like on a ladder,
So aim and smile because your life matters.
It's for you to blossom and not wilt,
To be successful you were built.

Medicine

It's a healing,
When your best you are not feeling.
It's a right on time remedy,
That gets you better quickly.
Its job it will do,
To get you back to being you.
It knows where to touch,
And soothe you so much.
When you hurt it eases the pain,
As needed a solution it will remain.
It's an aide,
To make the suffering fade.
It does its best,
Its action brings you rest.
Another feel, see and experience where you have been,
So their words, encouragement, support,
inspiration, and comfort are your medicine.

Fate

Sometimes we are afraid and fear to admit,
That we want and desire something or someone so bad every bit.
The bigger picture see,
It wasn't supposed to be an informality.
It's beyond our control,
It wants to show you the way by entering your soul.
It is your destiny,
And letting it be your eyes, ears and voice are the key.
You try to make it seem like it's not for you,
But thinking, dreaming, feeling, and
seeing this thing is all you do.
You do everything you can to cast it away,
But something about it reminds you of it every day.
It's meant to be,
It's the answer and solution it's trying to get you to see.
To achieve, change, gain, improve, accomplish, enhance,
grow, do over, make it right and sustain is never too late,
Because we are still here, being around each other,
having thoughts and still love because of fate.

Leap

Into what God has prepare,
Because it's happening soon as you are almost there.
To higher heights,
As God turn a negative into a positive, a bad
into a good, and a wrong into a right.
For a better day,
As you are on your way.
Into the abundance of more,
As you keep trusting, waiting, and walking into open doors.
Ahead for what awaits you,
Because the miracles and impossible God is about to do.
As you will advance,
And given another chance.
Your blessings and increase have arrived,
Because your winnings and manifest has come alive.
Your joy, love, happiness, and peace are yours
that you asked and prayed for,
Because it's your time and season to soar.
The time and year have come to reap,
So into your overflow leap.

Endure

In life difficulties you will face,
Before the winnings you embrace.
Everything comes with a price,
And there will be a sacrifice.
The denial, being crucified, shedding of blood,
nailed, and death Jesus went through,
So understand nothing will happen easy for you.
You must go through to receive,
That's why you have to pray, trust, and
wait, so you have to believe.
Have faith in the after,
You will be rewarded greatly with peace, joy,
life, happiness, love, and laughter.
Even when it gets hard don't faint, draw weary,
give up, or quit continue to preserve,
Because your blessings, overflow, season, and increase are near.
You must give and show works to be gifted,
As your prayers are lifted.
In what you go through won't last always,
So through it and before it happens start now
thanking God and giving Him praise.
You have to be still and know,
At the right time what's for you will show.
It is for you to be bless, to reap, and be favored for sure,
But the sufferings, pain, brokenness, hurt, troubles, obstacles,
challenges, trials, and tribulations you must endure.

Manifest

It's about to arrive,
Because it's for you to see and receive while you are alive.
It will come by surprise,
But it won't have a disguise.
What's for you is going to appear,
And God will make it clear.
Through it all faithful and humble you remain,
It's your time to gain.
For the wait,
God is going to make it great.
It's about to become obvious,
That it's for you to be victorious.
The favor is in your court,
Because you didn't give up so for what you asked
and prayed for God will answer and support.
Great is for you to have,
So at the enemy laugh.
Let there be a countdown,
Because what God is about to do in your life is
going to be mine blowing and so profound.
It's is coming your best,
And watch and see it manifest.

Win

Don't let the storms, hard times, trials,
challenges, and troubles distract,
Because of all of that you will gain it all back.
Your failures will produce,
Success for you to be introduce.
Embrace your season,
What occurred is about to speak and you will know the reason.
Get into position to receive,
Because blessings you are about to retrieve.
That you believe, trust, and wait, your overflow will be great.
It's for you to accomplish,
As you will finish.
So your prayers and desires set,
And in timing you will get.
You can't stop until you reach your destination,
So you can reap the release and manifestation.
Focus on where you are going and not where you been,
Because it's time for you to win.

Reverse

A bad to a good,
And God will do the impossible because
He is the only one that could.
A wrong to a right,
Because you continue to do good and in God delight.
A negative to a positive,
As you will see miracles and the goodness while you live.
Tears to joy,
And give you back what the enemy tried to steal, kill, and destroy.
From nothing to something, Because
what you ask God will bring.
From darkness to light,
Because you walked by faith and not by sight.
From that to this,
Because what was will be dismiss.
The sickness and generational curse,
Start thanking God because it's being reverse.

Tables Turn

You have been through a lot every bit,
Please believe me, you God didn't forget.
You are on the top of list for you He cares,
Your blessings He prepares.
What you thought couldn't be,
It's about to happen for thee.
What may have saddened you,
A shift and change God are about to do.
Watch God do this 360,
He said is there anything too hard or impossible for me?
Access granted it's yours,
For you God open doors.
God said make room,
They thought it was for them but it's for you, boom!!!
Your time is here,
You are about to win my dear.
God can do all things,
So try and pray about it again and watch what God brings.
You, the good and the enemy are eating at the same table,
But God is about to show you that He is able.
It's your time to earn,
Because for you the tables turn.

Expect

Favor to be on you,
Faith to see you through.
The enemy to be on your back,
But God has you so you won't lack.
That blessings you will receive,
And rewards to retrieve.
What's for you is on the way,
And answers when you pray.
The rain to produce from the mustard seeds,
And God is on time to meet needs.
Your winning season,
Everything happens for a reason.
Things to turn,
And your spirit to discern.
From a wrong you can correct,
So goodness and change expect.

Be Joyful

Let us be glad,
And not dwell in anger or become mad.
It's for us to be great,
And don't let life's struggles aggravate.
Don't live in your scorn,
You can always start over and move on.
Yes, things will come at you,
So focus on the getting through.
Smile more,
Don't let the enemy steal your joy so in positivity soar.
We will go through ups and downs,
But trust in God to turn things around.
Waking up each day is a blessing,
So in your troubles stop stressing.
Don't grumble or complain,
Because you still have life so humble remain.
From a storm there is a sunny day,
And what's for you will show up on time with no delay.
Have light and don't be dull,
So learn to be joyful.

The Storm

It brews a rage,
But you can turn the page.
Challenges, obstacles, and chaos at you it blows,
But be still as the peace, calmness, and serenity flows.
A lot of damage it can do,
As starting over stares at you.
It may cause a break,
But it's to get you right for your sake.
Can last a white,
But still smile.
Has many afflictions,
But victory is the prediction.
It's to create the true,
And bring forth something new.
That's when blessings form,
When you are in the storm.

Saturate

Let blessings flow like a flood,
And soak us Jesus with your oil and blood.
With love let us get drenched,
And by peace be quenched.
By wisdom we want to be infused,
And only you God we will choose.
Cause an overflow with your grace,
And let joy fill our face.
By faith let us get wet,
And the abundance you do daily for us we won't regret.
Hope on us rain,
As the harvest we gain.
In kindness let's soak,
As negativity, moodiness, hate and bad attitudes we provoke.
Every and anything about you is great,
As we allow you to saturate.

In Advance

Now I will rejoice,
Because God I heard your voice.
For the miracles to come my way,
To the answers to the prayers that I pray.
The blessings that are going to flow,
An increase suddenly will happen I know.
Unexpected rewards to see,
And what God has for me.
What's to come,
An overflow rewarded to me from where I came from.
For what I didn't think would be possible,
But God's timing is always right on time and His able.
Thru the pain, storm, struggles and troubles,
Seeing God blessing me with double.
In faith I will be,
As the plans reveals that is waiting for thee.
I will praise, shout and dance,
Thank you, God, in advance.

Everything

Is in your timing,
Just continue to keep climbing.
Is in your hands,
As by me you stand.
Is in your will,
I have learned to be patient and still.
Is in your plan,
I've mastered to trust you and not man.
Is in your season,
Because things happen for a reason.
Will be given back to me that was taken,
As me you never forsaken.
Will fall into place,
No matter what is faced.
Don't fear a thing,
God because of you are everything.

The Path

For me it is the plan,
By God and not man.
It was chosen for me,
So greatness and blessings I can see.
Designated for my view,
God, I thank you.
It's not an easy road,
But God is with me to carry the load.
With curves and being straight,
By faith I will get to my destiny the future God creates.
Along the way may be some diversions,
But the victory will be ton.
What's for me is on it,
It's for me to get thru it and not quit.
Just stay on it even thru the wrath,
It is destined for me the path.

Be Thankful For

The years God continues to give,
And enjoy every moment that we get to live.
The opening and closing of your eyes,
And the setting of the sun and when it rise.
The mountains God has moved,
And the mistakes and lessons learned to help you improve.
The few,
And in God's timing you will get your plenty and
cast away the old and welcome the new.
The storms, trials, failures, and your success,
And the pain, hurt, faith and test.
All the reasons to say thank you,
As we see others that are blind, deaf, mute, artistic,
lame, cripple, different types of handicaps and
challenged but great things they still do.
They don't let their disabilities stop them from
being and doing something great,
And we without a lament should not
complain and a humble spirit create.
As God gives, it's for us to give and do more,
So with everything be thankful for.

Just

Be a spark,
And be light to the dark.
Be happy every day,
And anticipate great things to come your way.
Know who you are,
And in life you can go far.
Be kind,
And free your mind.
Let peace consume you,
And a good deed always do.
Enjoy the life you are given,
And forgive, apologize, care, give flowers and
create memories while you are living.
Love more and more,
And dream big and soar.
Wear a smile,
And take steps to go the extra mile.
Learn to give,
And you will receive as long as you live.
As many times say I love you,
And spontaneous and for no reason something nice do.
Be fair,
Because it's a two-way street so with the one share.
Create laughter,
And what you want go after.
A move bust,
It's for you to just.

Suddenly

Blessings will flow,
And you will grow.
What you thought couldn't happen will,
All you have to do is be still.
What was lost will be found,
Just watch God turn things around.
Faith will appear,
Always in God timing my dear.
The walls will crumble,
Because you remained humble.
The burdens will fall,
Because God heard your call.
Things will come into place,
Because of mercy and grace.
The tears will dry,
Never doubt that God didn't hear your cry.
It will appear so fast,
That you won't have time to remember or dwell on the past.
Your soul and spirit will rejoice and be bubbly,
Because before your eyes miracles and the
impossible will start happening suddenly.

Don't Rush

The process,
Because with patience you will be bless.
What God is doing in you,
Just believe great things He is about to do.
Your time take,
And wise decisions make.
Nothing in life happens quick,
So with God's plan stick.
Take one day at a time and slow,
And go with the flow.
The closer you get you will see,
That waiting was the best option for thee.
It will happen when you least expect it,
So don't get impatient or quit.
Be still and hush,
God's timing don't rush.

Keep Walking

The journey may seem long,
You just don't give up or quit, so continue to be strong.
So have faith step by step,
Because God has great things in stored, He's your rep.
It's a distance away,
Continue the path you will see it in any day.
Just down turn or look back,
It's a process just keep straight on track.
The rewards and blessings are ahead,
Because God is able to do the impossible
that's why by Him you are led.
You may get tired but don't faint,
Because you will be very pleased with the reveal that God paints.
Your destination hasn't arrived just yet,
So don't stop your walk because what's for
you believe and trust you will get.
What God has promised and has been talking,
It will happen you just keep walking.

Speaking Out Loud

God, I will trust you all the time,
Even when I just have a dime.
You bless me in so many ways,
Even when I want to cry, get stress, feel frustrated and
just don't know, that's when I start giving you praise.
Family and friends, I can't look to you,
For me only God can do.
I'm going to make it,
So I can't quit.
God, I thank you,
For all you have done and will do because
the true honor to you is due.
I know better you have for me,
So I'm waiting on you so I can see.
Me and unconditional love will meet,
And it will come with many attributes to make me complete.
Your voice God I won't ignore,
Because you are in the blessing, making ways and
keeping promises as I will reap much more.
I will only go up,
As I will be debt free, do and have the best,
see the better and be that example of a miracle
as there will be an overflow in my cup.

My heart will make me receive,
Because I give of myself and in God I believe.
My talents are for others and I must display my gifts,
Because I have to encourage and inspire because I was
blessed with the power of someone' else's spirit to lift.
My name will be known,
And my creativity will be shown.
It's not just for me,
Those connected to me will also receive and see.
God, I will make you proud,
As my feelings and claim I'm speaking out loud.

This Is The Day

To be glad in,
And to make up your mind to win.
For the impossible to take place,
Rejoice now because of grace.
The victory will be yours,
As God opens up many doors.
You will get the good report,
God has you always, He is in your court.
That the tears you have cried will turn into joy,
And everything not of God will be destroyed.
It will come to pass your dreams and hope,
Because God has your blueprint and plan and, in His timing,
He will bless you for all the things that you cope.
To see how God moves, His wonders and way He will prove.
To watch God, show up and show out,
No need to doubt.
To let faith lead,
And your blessings, increase and overflow will
reward you from your mustard seed.
For the things you pray,
Just watch God because this is the day.

God Has The Last Say

We don't ever want to see someone sick or in pain,
But in our faith, we must remain.
When it's their time to take their final
rest we can't question why,
But it's ok to cry.
Life is something very strange,
And at any time, it can change.
We have to make sure that we do our part,
Care for, visit, love, make memories, bend, hold their hands, bring
warmth, call, give flowers and give your all from your heart.
Any burdens, hurt, pain and grudges forgive for and release,
Let there be peace.
A person departing this earth we don't want to think about,
But when it's their time we can't doubt.
It's for us to pray,
But God has the last say.

Trust

It can be a very hard thing to do,
But God I have to learn to give it to you.
As difficult as it may be,
A solution I will see.
I've worked so hard to build again,
And then come obstacles, storms and challenges
that's trying to bring me to an end.
It's like I've been in some situations too long,
But that's when my faith has to remain strong.
To every problem there is a solution,
I have to know that greater can come from pollution.
The right timing is always the key,
Waiting and staying positive has to become my capability.
Things may crumble and fall right in front of my face,
But every time I'm greeted, put together
and picked back up by grace.
Things good and bad will be done,
To get things right it only takes the Mighty One.
Just like dust I blow, for the unseen to happen I got to know.
As soil minerals and water makes clay,
Me and prayer has to know that God will make a way.
It's that mindset I have to keep,
And not get frustrated or worry just go to sleep.
It's like that mustard seed and it's very small,
I have to give nothing or my all.
Am I out or in,
The failures, hiccups and blood treads have to give
me the willpower and determination to win.
To believe with all my heart is a must,
As in God I trust.

Hope

Evidence to hold on to,
Encouragement does what it is supposed to do.
It may start out small,
Believing makes it grow tall.
Something to see,
Grasp it to help you on your journey.
To see better days,
In timing God will show you in many ways.
It's your light,
When you lose sight.
It's the thrive that motivates you,
It's the sign to see you thru.
Its purpose is for you to not give up never,
It was created to be with you forever.
Just don't fear,
It will reveal clear.
It's the addictive to make life better,
As with it storms you weather.
When life, challenges, tribulations, and obstacles you can't cope,
Just know you can rely on hope.

Surplus

You will experience it in excess,
Because of the favor on your life, you will be bless.
For you not giving up when things get tough,
You will receive more than enough.
An abundance God will supply,
For every tear you cry.
Believe it and expect it your overflow,
And what God's word says trust and know.
Your winning season is now,
And you will have leftovers to help and bless all those around.
For what you ask God will exceed,
Because you have faith in your mustard seed.
You will see the more,
And an increase explore.
To you God will multiply and add,
So rejoice and be glad.
Just say thank you Jesus,
For your surplus.

Shavetta Craig

I'm Not

Stopping until God is finish with me,
So I can't quit because blessings are ahead for me to see.
Going to worry,
I will praise and give God all the glory.
Going to let failures keep me from success,
It's for me to be bless.
Leaving until my full life I enjoy,
And what God has for me I will not let the devil destroy.
Throwing in the towel,
Or dwelling in sorrow.
Going to let trials way me down,
I'm depending on faith to turn things around.
Letting my peace, joy and happiness be stolen,
And no drowning in debt because it's for me to win.
I will give God and life all I got,
And giving up on trusting Him I'm not.

He Knows And Sees Your Heart

Wrong has been done,
But you help others so a good deed you did one.
It wasn't supposed to be touched,
But to other lives you gave much.
A bad can bring forth a good,
By being there for others as you should.
It's not a constant intention you do,
You just trying to see yourself and others get thru.
Even if damage unfolds,
What is seen is your good that is like gold.
From your mistakes no one can't judge,
But what stands out are your fruits that can't be smudged.
Guilty or not,
A giving spirit you got.
To have peace and happiness it sometimes makes
you do crazy and not so good things,
As harm to no one you don't want to bring.
Getting your hands dirty wasn't your art,
But God, He knows and sees your heart.

Get Our Attention

It's for you to follow,
As you get us thru tomorrow.
In our lives it's a stir,
As chaos around us occur.
We fall,
As you wait on your name for us to call.
Battles we face,
You wait to offer us your grace.
We keep going thru storms,
You want us to hear from you as blessings you are able to form.
To us troubles seems to last,
But you have all power to cast.
We keep looking and going in the wrong direction,
But the search is you who is our protection.
With all we go thru,
You are trying to get us to focus more on you.
Your will and your way continue to be mentioned,
God as you are trying to get our attention.

God Is

Awesome with all His might,
Marvelous and has a shining light.
Amazing in everything that He controls,
Zesty is His spirit and He saturates your soul.
Inventive as we are His creation,
Natural at bringing our lives a sensation.
Great and mighty is He.

My Soul Says Yes

I humble myself unto you,
Submitting my life is what I have to do.
I give you my all,
As I harken to your call.
By you I'm fed,
And also led.
My worship I give,
As for you I live.
Anything that is not like you; take it away,
Fill me with your spirit as to you I pray.
Please enter in, and cast away my sins.
You are in control, So have my soul.
You I seek,
As to me you continue to speak.
Today I'm free,
And I give you the victory.
I get into my private place,
So I can get before your face.
You are a need,
You are the potter and I am the clay and a seed.
I'm willing and ready,
To have you always and be steady.
When you knock, I will open the door,
So you can purify me and in my life soar.
I will need you forever,
My yesterday, today, tomorrow, and future endeavor.
To you I listen and am bless,
To Jesus my soul says yes.

We Need

You Lord first and foremost,
And peace to keep us on coast.
Faith to walk by,
And on grace rely.
Hope to lead the way,
And perseverance to display.
Joy to be a guide,
And mercy to provide.
A positive reflection to display,
And to always be kind and to pray.
Patience to wait,
And in God's timing He will make life great.
For another be there,
And have a spirit to give and care.
Encouragement to spread,
And wisdom and knowledge in our heads.
To stay true,
And faithfulness, greatness, and goodness view.
To be thankful every day,
And know that Jesus will make a way.
To learn to be humble,
Because life is imperfect, we will stumble.
Grateful to be our call,
And thank God for it all.
Happiness indeed,
And importantly love is all we need.

Build For Us

We have been through a lot,
But faith is all we got.
It's a process to go through,
But God has said trust I got you.
No more renting it's time for you and your family to have a house,
From your faithfulness, humbleness, thankfulness, and
gratefulness a place to call home will sprouse.
Patience became our anchor,
As the timing has come to soar.
Prayers are the masterpiece,
As we watch our blessings being release.
With the application we start,
God now it's your turn to finish it with your part.
What we ask, seek, and knock for we shall get,
Because the favor and glory of God are on our lives every bit.
The foundation, structure, frame, ceilings, doors,
fixtures, windows, floors, and location will be bless,
As it will be built in Jesus' name with success.
A new address to call home,
Each step of the way you are with us,
We didn't have to do this alone.
Thank you, Holy Spirit, Father, and Jesus,
As this home was built for us.

Breathe

The enemy wants you to crack,
By having you focus more on what's
going wrong and on your lacks.
The enemy uses your weakness to take control of your mind,
And of your fight, faith, trust, determination, not giving
up and belief in God the enemy wants you to be blind.
Yes, the struggles, pain and hurt are real,
But have the strength to move on and to heal.
Yes, troubles pile like an overload,
Believe and remember God will never
leave you or forsake you as told.
Keep your eyes on God and not the problem,
And in His timing God will solve them.
Even when it's not the enemy it's your own fault,
God will get you out of that too because He forgives
and forgets and still produce mighty results.
Don't let the enemy or you trying to take control of you,
Just know there isn't anything that God can't do.
You may be in a fog that clouds,
But keep walking by faith and not sight and it will
fade away so make God and yourself proud.
You can't take it anymore because failures,
doubt, fear, challenges, and obstacles are
drowning you like a downpour of rain,
Remember you must go thru to gain.

Not withdrawing from God, complaining, quitting,
throwing in the towel, not finishing, and letting the
enemy have the victory are the lessons to learn,
What God has promised in His word you will yearn.
In the flood of excuses, selfishness, self-pity, suicide, worrying,
anger, temperament, and sleepless nights from this swim,
Conquer and don't drown in them.
So inhale and exhale,
And let Goal prevail.
To your winning season cleave,
You got this so just breathe.

Pray Trust Wait

Let God hear your voice,
And what's for you will be His choice.
What you want to be answered say,
And keep believing every day.
Out loud, silent and with others do,
And watch God bring favor upon you.
On God depend,
And healing, deliverance and change He will send.
Leave it in God's hand,
And by His word stand.
You just have to know,
And let your faith grow.
Unexpectedly and on time it will be,
His miracles you will see.
In His timing things will manifest,
Your patience is the test.
Just because it's not happening right away don't quit,
Watch God work be still and sit.
Your happiness, joy, peace, love, and blessings God will create,
Just pray, trust, and wait.

Think

Before you speak,
And the right words seek.
Of how you can make a difference and
touch someone each and every day,
And the image that you betray.
When something should be done,
And following God who is the only one.
Of how another it will affect,
And mistakes are made every day,
so remember no one is perfect.
About how you would want to be treated,
And with a smile is how others want to be greeted.
How your demeanor makes others feel,
And what can you do to help someone else heal.
About what matters,
And fix the brokenness of a shatter.
Before you react,
Know all the details and be calm don't attack.
Things can happen with a blink,
So take the time to think.

Please

Love them more than you did before,
Even though they may keep failing let them know with
faith and continuing to try they will one day soar.
Truly be there for them,
And be their light when they are dim.
Have an open mind and heart,
By understanding, listening, and feeling is how it starts.
Look pass faults,
And produce a new outcome and positive results.
Let them know we all make mistakes,
They are lessons learned and they will make it and get a break.
Let them know they still have a dream and purpose,
It's right there ready and eager to come out and surface.
Help them see pass their situation and pain,
And ensure them that God is in control and they still can gain.
Show them to pray, trust, wait and release,
And thru anything they go thru they will have peace.
Say I love you;
You are somebody, you will make it, you can do it,
I'm proud of you and give them a high five,
But thru what they have been thru or going thru they
will conquer it because they are still here alive.
Give them a reason to smile,
And when you can for them go the extra mile.
Let them know there is another day and year,
Make things happen and embrace their fears.
Put their mind at ease,
And encourage, comfort, and support them please.

Remain

Always be humble,
Even when you stumble.
To others be kind,
And keep a positive frame of mind.
To the Lord stay faithful,
Because He is your light when you're dull.
To yourself be true,
And righteousness do.
A person giving,
With an inspiring living.
To God in love,
And be pure like a dove.
Dedicated and caring,
And of yourself sharing.
To God's will be steadfast,
And in your heart, mind, and soul let His endurance last.
In life be patient,
In God's timing your blessings will be sent.
Be positive and upbeat,
And it's with Jesus that makes your life complete.
Wisdom and knowledge obtain,
And in peace remain.

Created

To lend an ear,
And another's cry hear.
For other's pray,
And to ensure them that God will make a way.
To get to the surface,
To uncover their purpose.
To get others to smile,
And for them go the extra mile.
To share my heart,
And do what I can to do my part.
To motivate,
And let others know they are great.
To inspire,
And keep you from hells fire.
To love and embrace,
And to let you know that your life is full with grace.
To be positive,
And happy and grateful lives live.
To discern,
And show my concerns.
To make things calm, peaceful, and a good feeling anticipated,
That's why I was created.

Faith

Walking thru darkness knowing you will find light,
Knowing you are a winner so finish the fight.
Believing in the power of prayer,
Because it will get you there.
The road is not easy but you will finish,
Because you are wise and distinguish.
See yourself thru,
No doubting, believe in you.
You don't see how but you know there is a way,
So focus and determined stay.
Not knowing how to get out,
But trusting in God is what it's about.
Taking that step,
Knowing that by God you are kept.
Just go ahead and leap,
That's the chance you take to reap.
Challenges awaits the brain,
It's waiting on you to gain.
Learn to be courageous,
In your life go to the next chapter, turn the pages.
Finding Action In Transpiring Hope

Double

It means two,
And an overflow is going to happen for you,
Wisdom and patience you must retrieve,
And when you least expect it; the blessing you will receive.
When you are in your rightful place,
You will have favor, peace, happiness, joy, and grace.
Remember God wants to bless you,
So just do what He wants you to do.
Of you decrease,
So God can increase.
From the apartment to the mansion,
Create an atmosphere that will bring expansion.
And not wanting to serve God; you got the nerve,
He has to see that you are worthy of the
blessings you feel that you deserve.
From your pain, sorrow, hurt, and trouble,
Wait on God and be ready and expecting double.

Turn

Chaos into peace,
And watch God provide an increase.
Confusion into clarity,
And your dreams, desires,
and prayers become a reality.
An ask into a given,
As your gifts and talents are your purpose
and assignment for living.
Weakness into strength,
And you can do all things at any length.
Failures into a win,
Because the power, determination, and favor are the way to begin.
Fear into success,
Because it's for you to be bless.
A seek into a find,
And always keep love and hope in mind.
Doubt into confidence,
Because faith is the evidence.
A knock into an open,
As the best and better waits within.
Sorrow into joy,
Because what God has for you no one could destroy.
Mistakes into lessons learned,
As everything has a turn.

From The

Fruits of our labor,
We will have favor.
Rising and setting,
The overflow and increase we will be getting.
Goodness of our hearts,
As with love, kindness, and forgiveness are how it starts.
Cross to the grave,
A new beginning for us was paved.
Hurt and pain felt,
A healing will be dealt.
Blessings to manifest,
We will have the best.
Good to be the reward,
As what's for us we keep walking towards.
Faith as small as a mustard seed,
As the answered prayers will happen indeed.
Valley to the mountain top,
And the victory, glory, mercy, and grace on us won't stop.
Nothing is too hard to see,
As God will show us that He is God from the.

Grace

God's favor upon you,
Even when it's not deserving He still do.
It's that added measure,
That you want to treasure.
When you think things are about to crumble,
On you it stumbles.
When you thought you had nothing,
Here comes something.
It creates a shift,
And it's job is to lift.
It's that safety net,
Right on time so glad we met.
It's that humbleness and gratitude for another day,
And it's the thing you thank and ask God for when you pray.
Mercy helps it too,
It lets you know that God's looking out for you.
It saves you every time,
That's why thank you Jesus you chime.
It's a needed thing,
And because of it; it makes your heart sing.
Doubt, fear, and a worry it takes its place,
I'm talking about grace.

Now

It's waiting on you,
It's right in front of you boo.
Dreams need to leap,
It's time to reap.
No time to procrastinate,
Life is ticking, make it great.
No time for sitting,
And definitely no way you are quitting.
It's there for you,
Push it thru.
Production takes action,
Stay away from any distractions.
Make it happen,
Because you have it within.
Take God and your creation and do the impossible,
For your success only you are responsible.
Be a better you,
Don't worry about others just do.
Face the task ahead,
You can do this just make sure by God you are led.
Speak and strive,
So your destiny can come alive.
You have to get up from down,
And it needs to take place now.

Elevate

It's time to transition,
So you must get into position.
So get your mind right,
And let your victory be your sight.
Know to be wise,
So to your destiny you can rise.
To the next level go,
In yourself believe and determination show.
From the bottom to the top,
Keep going don't stop.
Continue to press,
And aim for success.
A leap of faith take,
Even through the falls and mistakes.
To God's mercy and grace hold,
So a brighter future can behold.
See the destiny ahead of you,
And know that getting to it is the virtue.
God wants to see you do great,
So know it's time to elevate.

Control, Alt, Delete

On you things and your past have a hold,
You have to move on and again be mold.
It starts with a transformed mind, heart, and soul,
And that means letting God take control.
A change you must learn,
As a new way of life, you yearn.
Regardless of the fault,
There is an alt.
Something different can take place,
And it can be done with grace.
Let the pain and hurt fade,
Because the price for you has been paid.
All you need is three,
The Father, The Son, and the Holy Spirit to consume thee.
Starting over again isn't hard,
Unlock your faith and let down your guard.
To give your life a makeover so it can be complete,
You have to do a control, alt, delete.

Overflow

I have to say it and believe,
And in God's timing I will receive.
To my life I will speak,
So a change can peak.
It is for me to proclaim,
And receive it in Jesus' name.
To this difference I will make it there,
I'm determined somehow and somewhere.
A transformation will take over me,
The results will be powerful and profound you will see.
I have nothing to lose,
Because I have a mighty God to choose.
I will see the day,
That mentally, physically, emotionally, financially, socially,
and economically an abundance in my life will display.
For it to happen I have to know,
That's how you grow.
This effect I declare,
As praying, faith, trust, and determination help me prepare.
My resilience will show,
As I continue to speak over my life an overflow.

Throw Out The Trash

On it put your finger,
And don't let it linger.
There is too much bad,
The worst you ever been or had.
It's time to truly think,
Because what has a hold on you truly stinks.
It's been around too long,
It's giving off fumes something strong.
You have to get rid of the toxic waste,
And no more repeats or copy and paste.
Heavy it will continue to get,
So lighten your load so in peace you can sit.
You mess is in an overflow,
Don't let it destroy you to your low.
you have to start over from empty,
And want a better you simply.
I'm tired of you getting bash,
So it's time to throw out the trash.

When You Are Overwhelmed

Start to pray,
And cast your burdens to God right away.
Know you serve a mighty God that will see you thru,
So trusting, believing, and having faith do.
You will have struggles, circumstances, and face things,
But a way out for you God will bring.
Don't let what's bothering you hold you down,
Let mercy and grace keep you sound.
Obstacles you will face,
But you are built strong to finish your race.
This is just a test,
So give God and yourself your best.
Hand it over to God and sleep at night,
And on happiness, peace and joy don't lose sight.
Just like blowing out a candle,
Know that it's handled.
Know theirs light to your dim,
When you are overwhelmed.

Torn

Between love or hate,
Being alone or being a mate.
If he or she, did you wrong or right,
But on what really matters you lose sight.
Should I stay or go,
Let it die or turn things around so love can grow.
Because you thought he or she abandon you,
Did you try, gave hope, changed, or said no what did you do?
Because you knew you treated them wrong,
But you take out your anger, frustration and blame on
them and expect them to continue to stay strong.
Between family or the single life,
Learning your good or keep dwelling in your strife.
To smile or cry,
Start again or say goodbye.
Things may have happened to make you scorn,
Turn bitter into better and no longer be torn.

Trust And Believe

Regardless of your mistakes made,
It's forgiven and your past will fade.
Don't focus on your situation,
Faith is your anticipation.
Faithfulness is to key,
To grant you the victory.
Yes it gets hard,
But don't quit or let down your guard.
Remain humble, strong, and pray because others needs you,
In their distress, being down, lost, and depression
you will have to bring them thru.
We all face stumbling blocks and sorrow,
But know that it can get better tomorrow.
Just because you can't touch or see,
Continue to know and walk because God will
guide you to where He wants you to be.
It's easier said than done,
Will you trust God or to fear and doubt run.
Don't let the looks and lacks get to you your best,
Give it to God and rest.
It's all about knowing,
And let God do the showing.
Yes it can break you,
But there is nothing for you that our God cannot do.
Patience will bless you to receive,
But you must trust and believe.

Boom

I can feel it,
Your blessing assurance is going to fit.
For your faithfulness, it is pay time,
The perfect timing of God is about to show
up and show out like a chime.
The blessings are going to appear like pow, pow, pow,
It will be so many that you are going to
say thank you Jesus and Wow.
His power is going to explode and crack,
And over your life in every area there will be no more lack.
It was lite but it tarried for a while,
It's happening now because from your pain, trials,
obstacles, circumstances, storms and challenges
God is ready to see you continuously smile.
All the suffering, hell, mistreatment, and
dilemma created in you a bomb,
Tick, tick, tick you are about to go off and an
atmosphere stir, change, turnaround, and shift
will take place at the sound of the alarm.
In your spirit God is brewing up a fire,
So you can fulfill and expose the purpose of His desires.
It's time to make room,
Because God is about to do some things in
your life that's about cause a boom.

The Way To Be

Be at peace,
And negativity around you cease.
Always be positive,
A smile, hug, and lots of love give.
Continue to keep going and be productive,
And don't put limitations on how to live.
Remember to every day pray,
Speak greatness and let inspiration and
encouragement lead the way.
Waiting is the key so be patient,
God's timing is perfect even when it seems ancient.
To the fullest your life live,
Enjoyment to you it wants to give.
Share and show love,
May it be pure and flows like a dove.
Every day laugh,
And fun always have.
Always be willing to learn,
As more wisdom and knowledge you yearn.
A purpose in life fulfill and happiness and joy see,
This is the way to be.

From Pain To Laughter

Yes it hurts bad,
And it has you mad.
It's a cycle that seems like it will never end,
Up then down, barely making it and then you see a
little light and then you love to be broken again.
Others did wrong you but some of your mishaps were your choice,
So be wise of what you voice.
Damaged, broken and confused,
But you still have what it takes to be used.
you have to free yourself from the attacks,
And no more looking, rewinding, reversing, or playing it back.
Greatness still comes from pain,
Regardless humble always remain.
Focus on God and you,
It's not about what people say, think, or do.
One minute you have it then it's gone,
Remove the daggers, dry the tears, and wipe up the
blood because you will heal from the scorn.
From consequences you pay a price,
But you will be dust off and polish and shine
bright like diamond pieces of ice.
You created all eyes to be on you,
You will always have an audience failure or success
show them that great things you still will do.

Yes you may be bitter,
Change that energy into a positive to become again a go getter.
The more hurt you go thru,
Will prepare you to soar and to yourself
find your identity and be true.
What God birth in you is priceless,
So continue to go after your success.
Still you don't see a way,
So still trust and believe unexpectedly God will
show up with your miracle any day.
Put your past experiences behind,
And for your dreams grind.
The hurt will turn into blessings after,
As you go from pain to laughter.

Turned Water Into Wine

It doesn't matter the view,
Jesus can make a difference in you.
All you have to do is ask,
In or out of season He can perform the task.
It's not about the drink,
It's the miracles He does that makes you think.
You could be one way,
And turned around as you pray.
It can take time or it can be quick,
But to His plan stick.
His your way maker,
And breath taker.
When you run out,
Who filleth you up without a doubt.
When you give Him more,
Into you He will continue to pour.
Jesus can make your life divine,
Just like He turned water into wine.

We Need

To love others more,
And continue to have manners, respect and
for the elderly and women open doors.
Jesus in our life,
It's the only way to see and to get rid of negativity and strife.
To constantly pray,
And live each day as if it's your last day.
To come together,
And produce results to make things better.
To have peace,
And be positive at least.
More helping hands,
And for righteousness stand.
More good,
And giving, sharing, and loving as we should.
A better tomorrow,
And stop living in these worldly sorrows.
Good than bad,
And people to be more happy than sad.
For kindness again to take power,
To remove the sour.
Justice for all,
And being a support when someone falls.
Prayer back in the school,
Because bullying and suicide isn't cool.
The right choice,
And to be heard by our voice.
Kind words to a heart to feed,
More greatness in this world we need.

Take The Back Seat

We try to do things on our own,
We need the Lord's help even when we are grown.
Every time we do it, we fail,
Let Jesus prevail.
The battle is not for us to fight,
It's the Lords so give it to Him as He guides you to the light.
It's too much for you,
The orchestrating let God do.
It's not for you to drive,
For God's wisdom, will and way strive.
You can let go and let Him take the wheel,
It's for Him to take control and deliver and heal.
God has a handle on things,
As greatness to you He brings.
God has you,
He wants His goodness, blessings, and
love for you to be your view.
For your life to be complete,
Let go and let, God and take the back seat.

It's The Remedy To Heal

When you are crush,
It's working it out so hush.
On it you can depend,
It has the power to mend.
When you are cut deep,
Lots of this you need to reap.
It's that aid,
When hurt invades.
When pain destroys,
This brings joy.
When you bleed,
It's that unconditional seed.
When you want to cry,
Your tears it dries.
When you are scorn,
It removes the painful thorns.
When your heart is split in two,
It's built, to put back together, that's what it will do.
When you feel blue,
It brings comfort to the rescue.
It soothes the aches,
And comfort it makes.
When you are sick,
To you it sticks.
Better it will always make you feel,
Love it's the remedy to heal.

A Time For Everything

Everything happens for a reason,
And it has its season.
And a timing for a purpose to come about,
Just have faith and don't doubt.
There is a time to be born and die,
To smile, live, and cry.
Your harvest plant, and pluck them when God grants.
It comes a time things to kill,
But we have to learn to be still.
Good we may not always feel,
But it is a time to heal.
Storms and tribulations will surround,
That will cause you to break down.
The time will come to build up,
So God can filleth up your cup.
There will be a time to weep,
But joy you will reap,
You will mourn,
But you will have the strength to move on.
Good times you will have,
With time to laugh.
A time to dance,
Because of your second chance.
A time to cast away stones,
So things can flee and be gone.

But you will have to gather those stones together,
To create something for your life better.
You will need to and not embrace,
Just be covered with grace.
There will be a time to get and lose,
That's for God to choose.
You will have a time to keep and cast away,
Just stay in God's will and pray.
A time to mend,
And time apart spend.
A time to sew,
Because mending you know.
There's a time to be silent and to speak,
So discernment seek.
A time to love and hate,
But you can create a clean slate.
Timing for war and peace,
Let the chaos cease.
For your labor,
What do you do for your Savior?
What God giveth He can take,
So do right for His sake.
Beautiful things God made in His time,
And He set the world in their heart to chime.

There is no good in them,
But for a man to rejoice and to do good in
his life, even through his dim.
And every man should eat and drink and enjoy the
good of all his labor his spirit should lift,
From God this is a gift.
What God doeth will be forever, so nothing can be put
in or taken from it catch that in the spiritual rim,
That men should fear before Him.
Your has been is now and God require that which is past,
The same God right now is the same God
back then, so Him don't cast.
You inner spirit feed,
So Ecclesiastes 3:1-15 please read.

Second Chance

To reverse your mistakes,
And mend the heartbreaks.
To love right,
And let sustaining, thriving, staying together
and endurance be your guiding light.
To prove that you can do better,
And storms weather.
To give and do your best,
And put bad habits to rest.
To hold your head high and not fear,
And hold on to the one that has your back and for you cheer.
To vow again,
And keep them this time my friend.
To command obstacles and challenges to move,
And that you are great and faithful prove.
To live the life you should,
And your all do you could.
Get close without the distance to rebuild love,
friendship, and romance,
So thank God for a second chance.

Stay

With family and friends connected,
And keep them and yourself protected.
In a frame of mind that is positive,
And enjoy life and live.
hurting at home,
And in these streets don't roam.
To others kind,
And see again from being blind.
In the know,
And continue to grow.
With family committed,
And with love don't quit on it.
In a great mood,
And lose the negative attitude.
In your lane,
Be focus, mind your business and be who you
are and keep things simple and plain.
In good spirits and always pray,
On a good note, stay.

Walk Into The Goodness

The time has come to reset,
And your former completely forget.
A new path has been made,
What was holding you back, hindering you,
hurting and broken you let it fade.
It's time to come to grips,
You must become a better you and with favor,
mercy, and grace you are equipped.
It awaits you,
Just walk on thru.
You have endured much pain,
So your reward for your faithfulness blessings you will gain.
The wicked and negativity wants revenge
and wants to take over you,
But you have to be strong and the good do.
Dust yourself off and get back up,
God is about to pour an overflow into your cup.
Don't waiver,
Know that you have favor.
Your healing, deliverance and victory is a straight shot,
What do you have to lose give your
destiny and journey all you got.
For your storms and troubles,
Be alert, take heed and pay close attention because
your blessing portion will be double.
God wants to give you more not less,
So walk into the goodness.

When Needed Most

When there was nothing,
I did what I had to do to create something.
When others failed you,
Until this day I remain solid for you and still do.
Even with your secrets, pride, and the things you hide,
I forgave and still provide.
When things you lost,
I woman up and did for us at all cost.
When you were down to your last,
I stepped in and made things again a blast.
When you were at your low,
With my being, love and life I helped us grow.
Even when you faded,
I was still there for us I made it.
When there was no trace,
I still believed that change we will embrace.
Even when you strayed away,
I've always made myself available until this day.
Even when you didn't want to talk,
From your life I never walk.
When you wanted to trade,
My love for you never fade.
I'm the ride or die that is still on coast,
I'm the one who has been there from beginning
to end there when needed most.

Lesson Learned

To not hold back,
And to be a solution and not a problem to the lacks.
To keep things between me and you,
And the past things done that were not right don't continue to do.
When to be silent,
And don't let your anger and words become violent.
To keep family and friends out of your personal life,
And always work towards be a better person, husband, or wife.
When you're angry be careful of what you say,
Because words can destroy just take the time to pray.
Be considerate of each other's emotions and feelings,
And always let love be the healing.
That right is right and wrong is wrong,
And it's about striving, staying together, and becoming strong.
Don't let temptations and addictions take control of you,
And telling lies don't do.
Even thru a mess,
You can get out and be bless.
Being a useful, better, and defiant person, I have yearned,
As from my failures, mistakes, and wrongdoings a lesson learned.

Cleaning Up Your Act

Yourself you took the time needed to find,
And sit back and reflect to get yourself
in a different frame of mind.
What was done you want to correct,
And this time show and give the proper and upmost respect.
What was done you let go,
To make it work this time you know.
You are remorseful for the pain,
So you distance yourself because that
way you don't want to remain.
You don't want to continue to hurt the one you love,
How to be the person you are to be is the
change you are thinking of.
To do what you do,
You know that's not you.
You draw a conclusion to figure out,
To make things right don't doubt.
The new you explore,
Because inside you is much more.
Tears and a broken heart you no longer want to see,
So a better person you are determined to be.
You want to show improvements and make an impact,
As you are cleaning up your act.

Thru Your Mess

It's become a struggle for you,
To get to your destiny and view.
You think you know what's best,
But trusting God is the test.
You keep making the same mistakes,
The cycle break.
You rely on the wrong things to be your comfort,
Make change an effort.
Some unnecessary storms you had to weather,
Others care and just want you to do and become better.
You see the light,
But your fears, pride, past, hurt, rejections, emotions and
that dark place are stopping you from doing right.
People you don't have to please,
Let peace, joy, happiness, and you being proud of you be your ease.
Let love, love you back,
And stop letting past relationships and pain on you attack.
With your lacks come up with a solution,
And don't get stuck and caught up in your
own selfishness and negative pollution.
Yes, you created this,
But God can and will dismiss.
Use your energy this time to produce results,
And stop focusing on your faults.
Starting again and making better choices is not hard,
Pray, trust, believe and wait for your
timing so put down your guard.
Stop wrestling with your flesh,

And let God mold a new image in you fresh.
Don't dwell in a certain image to uphold,
Let who you are created to be unfold.
Damage and harm to you was done,
But you will live to give your testimony of how
you made it believe me you are the one.
Many things have happened to you that
could have caused your death,
But God, He said not yet because you still have purpose,
so it's not time for you to take your last breath.
In your emotions, self-pity, anger, doubt
and in quitting don't dwell,
Send those spirits back to hell.
Stop living and being who you are not,
Instead, be thankful, grateful, and humble
for the small or big that you got.
Be wise,
And when it's your time you will rise.
What you say promise to do,
And watch God bless you.
And don't say you are going to do it God's way,
Stick with His plan from it don't stray.

Of your past don't talk,
Because God gave you the strength from it to walk.
Don't run anyone away,
Be thankful for them and listen they just
want to help you day by day.
Now everyone is wrong,
From your demons don't let them make you
weak fight back because you are strong.
You have so much potential and work to do,
So make it happen because love, great health,
opportunities, and peace are waiting for you.
It's time to catch up,
Because God is waiting on you to fill up your cup.
It's not the time to get in your feelings,
Forgive, forget, and move on with your healing.
God will still use you and bless,
Even thru your mess.

We Shall See

Bad to become good,
And operate as it should.
Old can be created new, to produce great things for you.
A malfunction will transform, and quite the storm.
Darkness turns into light, and see a wrong reset to do right.
A delay seek progress, and produces success.
The impossible will be done,
Just trust and watch God the Mighty One.
The cease of gossip and chatter,
And prove that anyone can change and make life and love matter.
How errors can be corrected,
And mistakes are lessons learned to be perfected.
That maintenance is to improve,
And given the chance in the right direction to move.
Testimonies to be told, as this time the best unfolds.
Rust branded to shine,
And what was it was and now things will be fine.
The repair, and being fair.
Things turn around,
And getting back up from being knocked down.
Brokenness rebuilt, and freeing yourself from guilt.
Crumbles become whole,
And seeing a refresh mind, heart, and soul.
Sadness to create smiles, and forgiveness to carry you for miles.
Evidence of what God can do is the proof,
As faith covers you like a roof.
The greater for you to be, we shall see.

Forgive Me

For the wrongs I will do in advance,
As you always give me another chance.
Of my bad thoughts,
And any harm to others I brought.
For my sins, and the demons I fight within.
For my mistakes, and the heartbreaks.
For the damage I did, and of the bad habits that are hard to rid.
For the people I've shamed,
And pointing blame.
For not giving as I should,
And not loving as I could.
For making someone cry,
And giving up before I try.
For not dwelling in your presence as needed each day,
And not spending more time to pray.
For the not so good that I speak,
And allowing things to make me weak.
For not having a listening ear, and having doubts and fears.
For not letting faith be my sight,
And staying in darkness instead of walking into the light.
For the caused harm,
And not letting your guidance be my warning alarm.
For the lies told, and the unrighteousness that unfolds.
For the things I continue to hold on to,
Instead of releasing them to you.
For the guilt I feel, and of my past so I can heal.
A release, change, improvements, a fresh start, and your guidance
I'm ready to see, for everything Lord please forgive me.

A New You

The same old things you can't continue,
Switch up like the different choices on a menu.
That good thing it's in you deep,
It's waiting to be release so let it leap.
It's time to become wise,
And let the new definition of you rise.
Where would life take you just follow the
journey where you end up no one knows,
So let the hinderance that's holding you back be exposed.
Dust off and start again,
Because from any situation you can mend.
Chances you are given,
So be a great you while you are living.
Put away the games,
And live up to your character and your name.
Want to do right,
And let your darkness be exposed to light.
Better you can be,
And it's something to see.
The bad you use to do,
Change it and let God create a new you.

Show What You Are Made Of

Display what to expect,
The warmth, tenderness, love, loyalty,
trust, and the upmost respect.
You were established to blast,
And created to build a lifetime and to provide a blast.
To give a charm,
And a healing when in your arms.
A lead to endure the whole process,
And because of your faith and determination
what you form will be bless.
An answer to a prayer,
And doing whatever is possible to be there.
Your hope will guide you to the end,
And the great things that occurs after we become friends.
Actions and emotions to captivate the mind,
And produce something that is rare to find.
Give rewards to the heart to entice,
That everything about you is honorable, genuine, and nice.
Doing things unexpected, with thoughtfulness
and not of the norm,
As everlasting forms.
Because of what God has created in you
will let someone else fall in love,
So show what you are made of.

For A Moment

Tears I will cry,
Then joy will come to make them dry.
Don't focus on the tribulations, obstacles,
struggles, and your from,
Just know that the best is yet to come.
You will have storms,
But blessings will form.
Your troubles may keep you up not to sleep,
So rest because in God's timing you will reap.
There may be chaos around you,
But God will see you thru.
The bad and ugly will stir,
But your victory will occur.
It will seem like hell chimes,
But God always show up on time.
Pain you will feel,
But the unneeded layers God will peel.
You may feel discomfort for a while,
But again, you will smile.
Distractions release,
But you will have peace.
It's for us to go thru but get pass the torment,
It will just be there for a moment.

It's In Me

To remain faithful,
And to have light and not to be dull.
To be patient and wait on God's timing,
As His mercy and grace keeps me chiming.
To love,
And for others to go the extra mile and beyond and above.
To give,
And let joy, peace, happiness, and goodness live.
To be humble and let it sustain,
As thankful and grateful I will always remain.
To make a difference,
As I dwell in the Lords presence.
Great and wonderful gifts,
As I use it to encourage, comfort, support, inspire and uplift.
To be great,
As a rewarding image in me God creates.
To be an example and lead,
And touch those in need.
To be a queen,
And to have faith in the unseen.
A spirit that is inviting,
As reaching others with my cooking, my smile, and my writing.
To be the best I can be,
As favor too it's in me.

No More Worries, No More Pain

How will I pay the bills,
God it's your will.
This situation how will I come out,
The name of Jesus shout.
This habit, affliction, addiction, and
temptation have a stronghold on me,
Jesus died for your sins so set free you will be.
I made the wrong choice,
Listen for God's voice.
Wrong decisions I continue to make,
God is still with you He will never leave you or forsake.
True love is so hard to find,
Wait on the Lord because love is patient and love is kind.
I battle with myself my inner man,
Trust God for you He has a plan.
Why am I here,
For you I have a purpose and I know the thoughts
for you said the Lord so don't fear.
Why can't I see pass this,
Have faith and your doubts dismiss.
Brokenness and troubles always seem to follow,
Hope, mercy and grace will lead you into tomorrow.
The pieces will come together,
And things will get better.
Believe in your blessings, Gods promise, and your gain,
And there will come a day when you will
have no more worries, no more pain.

Fill The Void

We want to see things a certain way,
But there is power when we pray.
Alone we don't want to be,
But the answer is to wait on thee.
We seem to endure the same,
God, please know our name.
Disappointments occur,
What is love it's a blur.
Sacrifice and time we put in,
Why do we always follow sin.
We hope, have faith, and don't ask for much,
By your power and strength can we be touched.
We see right but there is wrong,
Help us to stay strong.
We were broken by loved ones,
As we want better for our daughters and sons.
We have so much lack,
And by our past and negative thoughts we are attack.
Memories aren't always fond,
Let forgiveness be our bond.
We battle with things that we can't control,
Lord bring peace, happiness, joy, and your presence to our soul.
Why does this keep happening to me,
Light, endurance, a continuous smile, goodness, everlasting
and faithfulness we deserve to have and see.
Lord let us trust you and not get annoyed,
As you fill the void.

As Long As I Live

I will teach,
How love can reach.
I will have faith and take a chance,
And provide kindness, laughter, and romance.
I will show how to love others and you,
Great and positive things do.
Create a life that is pleasant,
And be wonderful and triumphant.
Make a difference,
And making others happy a lifetime existence.
And put peace and joy in the forefront,
And prove that love can't be stunt.
Make a smile stay,
And have a positive attitude every day.
Do all I can,
And follow God's plan.
To help you,
And the greatness in you view.
Share the beauty that I possess,
And how that I'm bless.
To always stay and be thankful, grateful, and humble,
And pray for others because no one's perfect because
we all have challenges and stumble.
What's in me I will offer and give,
As long as I live.

Shavetta Craig

Don't Wavier

How did we get here,
Confused, distanced, estranged, broken and
our minds drifting over there.
Will we break,
Or a change and sacrifice make.
The care is not there as much,
Did you forget how your heart I touch?
Death is supposed to be the end,
Healing you should send.
The focus has gotten blurry,
We are fading what are you going to do hurry.
Too much was put into this,
We are supposed to come together like a fist.
The heart see,
And let yours beat for me.
The bleeding stop,
And the hinderance drop.
For the tears that fall,
Give mending your all.
Preserve what we have, it's a connection to savor,
And on our love don't wavier.

Be At Peace

You weren't created to be stress,
You are a gift so be bless.
My presence is to keep you calm,
By the world don't be alarmed.
Here is my hand,
By you I will forever stand.
Thoughts of me will keep your mind clear,
So do not fear.
What I offer and bring,
No man can do the same thing.
Wisdom, love, strength, and endurance I give to you,
What can the world do?
Don't let problems, obstacles, and difficulties in your heart stir,
Let your belief, trust and faith in God occur.
Have confidence and don't fear,
And let mercy and grace in your life steer.
Peace was granted unto you, the price was already paid,
John 14:27 says: Peace I leave with you, my peace I give you.
I do not give to you as the world gives.
Do not let your hearts be troubled and do not be afraid.
Of everything release,
And be at peace.

Doing What's Right

To God we pray,
But in our ways, habits, and negativity we stay.
Change we ask to see,
But we say there's nothing wrong with me.
Everyone else needs to do better and improve,
But you stay stubborn, in the same position and
don't make any type of effort to move.
God can tell you to do this,
You hear but the words you dismiss.
He can show you a sign or two,
It's revealed but you act like it's not for you.
We want to do our own thing,
When God is trying to supply you as peace, love,
happiness, blessings and favor He brings.
We say we want someone or something good but some of us don't,
Because when God says, shows and gives it to
us, we act blinded and to do we won't.
It can slap us in the face,
And still what is given we don't embrace.
We get so caught up in I or me,
That we can be selfish and not acknowledge the
rewards of greatness and a gift in another to see.

Into our ways we are so content,
Shake that off, renew your mind, regenerate your spirit,
and resuscitate your heart when a new direction is sent.
Sometimes all it takes is to make some corrections,
Because we fall short, we fail, we sin, and we
have storms we are not perfection.
The right things we sometimes ignore,
When it's right there in our faces, in our minds
and hearts and right at the door.
Let's regain our sight,
And get back to doing what's right.

We Ready

For something new,
Opportunities, beginning, elevation and the plan God
has for us and the promise He will now do.
For our faith walk,
As we believe and listened for you Lord to talk.
To make the next move,
As what we ask, seek, and knock you will prove.
For the horizon ahead,
Because our steps are ordered and by God we are led.
For the goodness, greatness, and the glory,
Because God is still writing and rewriting our story.
For what's next,
We were being prepared for this it's in the word the text.
For the blessings on blessings to receive,
Because we didn't quit, we continued to believe.
To see what we have been patiently waiting for,
As what was promised we will receive that and more.
We have been faithful, praying, humble, grateful,
thankful, patient, still and steady,
So for our next destination, purpose and season we are ready.

Won't He Do It

Show up right on time,
Feed you and fills you up at a drop of a dime.
Your life save,
Because His life He gave.
Guide you in the right direction,
And will be your protection.
Change that situation right before your eyes,
After your many tries.
Clear your name,
And of you He won't be shame.
Make you great,
And gives you a new beginning like the number eight.
Make you whole,
Because the power He beholds.
See you thru,
Have faith, trust, and believe in Him is all you have to do.
Get you from out of that pit,
So won't He do it?

I Know He Will Do It

No matter what comes up against me,
My Lord is there to save and rescue thee.
When financial burdens continue to attack,
God is on time and brings me thru, He has my back.
When I trust and believe in Him,
Favor, grace, mercy, blessings and increase
He provides when I'm out on a limb.
When I walk into light but the enemy
tries to cast me into the dark,
My faith and power in me God sparks.
Wrongdoings and deceit are trying to take my children out,
But my God heals, delivers, and set free so
them coming out I won't doubt.
Prayer truly changes things,
For my faithfulness goodness and greatness God will bring.
You must laugh in the enemy's face,
Because of God you are a conqueror and winner
so His strength and willpower embrace.
I don't care how many times troubles, storms
and tribulations come at me and you,
There is nothing that our God cannot do.
Bring it, me the enemy can't defeat,
I'm clothed with righteousness, the blood, and the spirit of
God from the crown of my head to the sole of my feet.
I will not doubt my God with what I see,
Because as long as I trust and have faith as a size of a
mustard seed He will always and forever have me.
So the troubles, challenges and obstacles will come and
go because God is always on duty He never quits,
Because seeing me thru anything I know He will do it.

Staying Alive

Life can be a struggle,
And with faith and with what we see we tuggle.
Situations and problems continue to surface,
But we have to remember that we are still here for a purpose.
Troubles don't last always we know,
So like a flower we will blossom and grow.
We have to take it day by day,
And we must always pray.
Know that things can change,
Even when it seems strange.
Life is not an easy task,
But in goodness, the best, better, and
living God wants us to bask.
Always give it all you got,
And persevere and give your best shot.
Life is not about giving up so continue to thrive,
While staying alive.

Shavetta Craig

Cover Me

With love to give,
And the purpose to live.
With the hope to endure,
And spreading joy and happiness for sure.
With peace to sustain,
And humble remain.
To stand out and not fit in,
And letting others know it's for them to win.
To light up to the day,
And know with God there is a way.
With a blessing that others can receive,
And let me be the reason that in you God they believe.
That your presence on me that others see,
So with a residue cover me.

The Slumber Is Over

Don't rest too long,
And don't continue to do wrong.
What God has for you don't snooze,
So the better choose.
To receive the good and great,
You can't be lazy or procrastinate.
Wake up and be wise,
And tell the Lazarus in you to rise.
You just might miss it if you continue to nap,
So into destiny tap.
On faith don't sleep,
It's how you get your blessings to reap.
From that situation, bed, chair, and from fear make a move,
Because in your life a point God is trying to prove.
You can't be dosing off because attention you have to pay,
Because God's timing can be in any day.
So be vigilant and be sober,
Because the slumber is over.

Shavetta Craig

When We

Fall short,
Faith is in our court.
Over time stray away,
God forgives and accepts us back any day.
Become blind,
Wisdom again find.
Doubt and fear,
Know that God is always near.
Going through storms, troubles, tribulations, and lacks,
Continue to trust God and what you lost and
from the past you will be rewarded back.
Let the spirit in us dwell,
God makes a way for us out of the prison,
fire, den, pit, death, and hell.
See what God is going to do,
We will allow the breakthrough.
Cast away the old for the new we can see,
Then better things will happen when we.

No Matter

What they say,
I will win anyway.
What I don't see,
I will continue to pray and have faith because God got me.
Of the low balance in my bank account,
God will favor me with substantial large amount.
What I go through,
Miracles for me God will do.
What it looks like I can't go by,
Because on God I must rely.
How long it takes I will continue to trust and believe,
Because what's for me in God's timing I will receive.
What the day brings,
Thank you God I will always sing.
How hard it gets,
I will not give up or quit.
Of my past, hurt, pain, brokenness, or shatter,
I will still come out on top no matter.

In Your Hands

The challenges, hardships, and storms that I go through,
It's for me to release them to you.
For me who is meant to be,
When the time is right him,
My worries and my frets, I will see.
Because me you didn't and won't forget.
My daily walk and day,
I let you lead the way.
When let I get anxious, fear, or doubt,
You're in control to figure it all out.
My children I put into your care,
So be with them everywhere.
My life I give,
As you give me a reason and purpose to live.
Everything that I pray for,
And I wait for you to make it happen and provide
the pour, open doors, and so much more.
When life gives me lemons and limes,
You show up and show out and prove to me that you are God
and you perform the impossible and miracles every time.
I give to you everything,
As calmness, serenity, and peace to me you bring.
The why, how, when, and what I don't understand,
Lord, I leave it in your hands.

It Changes Things

It is heard even when you think it is not,
Because the blessings for you God got.
Do it for you and especially for others too,
And watch and see what God will do.
It will be answered at the appointed time and hour,
So dwell in faith and let the worry and fear devour.
It can be said silent or out loud,
As it honors God and makes Him pleased and proud.
It will come through for sure,
Just make it a habit to do it more.
Believe and trust in it,
And on it don't quit.
It has to be constant,
And wait for it to happen because it's not going to be instant.
When you do it leave it with Him,
And do it when things are going well
and when it is dark and dim.
It's the way to God to talk,
And in what you ask in it walk.
Leave it in His hands and let His will be done,
Because it will be worked out by the Mighty One.
There is power when you pray,
So make sure that you do it daily every day.
As the miracles and manifestation, it brings,
So know that prayer it changes things.

Only God Can

Have the final say,
And meet us where we are at when we ask and pray.
Turn a situation around,
And what was lost, make it found.
Shed on us light,
And make anything right.
Make the impossible, possible,
And do many wonders while being invisible.
Have the power to restore,
And going above our expectations and giving us so much more.
Make us over from the old to something new,
Because nothing is too hard for Him to do.
Answer prayers,
Because for us He cares.
Make a way,
So stick with His plan and timing and don't stray.
Change man,
Only God can.

What Faith Really Is

Believing in what you can't see,
Knowing it's going to come through for me.
Not knowing the outcome,
And my God is where the miracles come from.
Having the patience to wait,
As the breakthrough I anticipate.
Trusting that it will happen in the timing right,
And following the guiding light.
Going after the impossible,
And knowing that God is able.
Having confidence that the blessings are on the way,
And the answer to what you pray.
Seek the plan that is His,
Living on hope is what faith really is.

It's Knocking At Your Door

The blessings that await,
And the opportunities that are going to make your life great.
The manifest on the horizon,
And your season to win.
The overflow and increase,
And the needed peace.
The joy to endure,
And following happiness for sure.
Your success, breakthrough, turn around,
comeback, and for you to soar,
And it's there too your elevation and so much more.
The answer to your prayers,
And the one for you who cares.
Love that wants to captivate you,
And this time it will sustain, fulfill, and stay true.
Potentials to see,
And a dream becoming a reality.
Your future,
And the Holy Spirit revealing to you the bigger picture.
The best and the good,
And everything happening as it should.
God so in your life He will continue to pour,
What's been chasing you it's knocking at your door.

When You Wanted To

Give up on everything,
Then blessings God brings.
Say I'm done,
But you have to continue to have faith
and trust in God the only One.
Shout enough is enough,
But you hear a voice saying it will get easy after
you weather the storm, the hard, trials, tribulations,
suffering, troubles, and the rough.
Speak it's not worth it,
But remember it's for you to win so you can't quit.
Explain with this I can't cope,
You can do it just have faith, love, and hope.
Throw in the towel and stop,
Your fears, doubts, worries, and unbelief you must drop.
Just cry, Joy will come so continue to try.
Stop believing,
In God's timing blessings you will be receiving.
Let go, God spoke and said no.
Believe it's never going to happen for me,
God reminds you that He is the same God
right now that He was back then,
He will do it again watch and see.
Be discouraged that there is no way,
As unexpectedly and suddenly God shows up and
shows out when you consistently pray.
The miracles and the impossible God will do,
Because He is always right on time when you wanted to.

About To Do Something

Give answers to prayers,
God is showing that He cares.
Showing you who His,
The thank you is all He is.
Big for you to see,
As miracles and the impossible are happening for thee.
A reality to view,
You are about to get your breakthrough.
Spectacular and great,
You will be glad that you did wait.
Amazing to be proud of,
And create, establish, and build love.
That you never expect,
And what is wrong, bad, and negative He will correct.
That no one else could do,
This God did it, shocking, unexpected, suddenly,
and surprising moment is all for you.
That doesn't feel or seem real,
Because the time has come for you to heal.
To make your smile stay,
Because more than you asked for is on the way.
Blessings into your life God is about to bring,
So have faith and believe that God is about to do something.

There Is No One

Greater than you,
Because of all the things for us that you do.
That loves us more,
And provides, protects, and open doors.
That comes before thee,
You are the I Am and the awesome one to see.
Like you to always have our back,
And take care of our lacks.
Name to call,
And to you we give our all.
Mighty enough of His title,
As in our lives He is vital.
That can give us peace,
And blessings on us release.
Worthy like Jesus the Son,
To compare to Him there is no one.

Show Us Why

We had to wait,
So we could receive what you have for us what is better and great.
Things took place,
Because you wanted to fill us with favor and grace.
There was storms, tribulations, and troubles,
Because you want to bless us with double.
Your timing is perfect,
So our own understanding and ways you had to reject.
We had to endure problems,
Because you were testing our faith and trust in you because
you have given us the strength to overcome them.
With some situations we had to cope,
Because you never want us to give, quit, or lose hope.
We had to go through,
So we won't boost and know that you deserve
all credit and honor that is to you.
We have to pray,
So in your will we will stay.
We fall and rise, been broken and put
back together, and hurt but heal,
As your power and blessings on us you reveal.
Love is always to be shown and given,
And the purpose for our living.
The old had to die,
God, you had to show us why.

Live In Joy

No negative thinking,
And in your sorrow and pain don't be sinking.
Giving up you can't do,
There is so much for you to live for your
strength is waiting on you.
The burdens from your heart release,
And fight and have peace.
God has the last say,
So pray, trust, believe and have faith every day.
Don't let what you are going thru get the best,
Just rely on God, get better and rest.
I'm not going anywhere,
For you I'm there.
Look at you and see a winner,
Get you back so start again as a beginner.
Smile, laugh, dream, live and have fun again,
You can do this the time has come for you to mend.
On you I want to count,
So listen and hear me with every amount.
Encouragement to you I will always feed,
And I got you indeed.
Of your situation you take control,
And let recovery and healing fill your soul.
Cry it's okay,
Let it all out and then let your smile show right away.
What you see don't let it destroy,
Just look to and live in joy.

Shavetta Craig

Let You

Be the start of our day,
Because you know the plan and you are the way.
Do it and fix it,
It's just for us not to quit.
Do your will,
As we just be still.
Take the lead,
As we trust in you indeed.
Move on our behalf,
And let us experience the live, love, and laugh.
Take control,
And do a new thing to our hearts, minds, and souls.
Show us that you are real,
And signs and wonders to us you will reveal.
Release the blessings for us to view,
So God, we must let you.

On My Behalf

God is working it out,
So in advance I will praise, thank Him, and shout.
What I speak I will see,
Because it's happening for me.
The winnings are proclaimed, and it manifests when
I say Amen, Hallelujah, and in Jesus' name.
God has placed me in a position to receive,
Because for me this is a long time coming
and I trusted, waited, and believed.
God said to bless you, it's time,
It wasn't a delay, He knew I would be ready in my prime.
God is showing me that the moment now is right,
He wanted to see that I can put others before myself to
use my gifts and talents to reach them with my light.
Love will be given and shown,
And blessings will be granted to me from places,
people, and territories unknown.
God will reveal,
That He is the real deal.
God is going to present to me things I didn't even ask for,
And will deliver what I prayed for and so much more.
The miracles and impossible for me are all around,
As the turn, shift, elevation, leveling up, rise,
and move are going to be so profound.
It's for us all to win,
Prosperity for the ones that I don't know, friends, and kin.
I passed God's test,
As I put my needs last to help others to their best.
What I patiently waited for my live, love, and laugh,
As God is so good because He is doing it on my behalf.

The Journey Of God's Plan

With the dilemmas of life you get hit,
But you can't quit.
You try to do things on your own,
You say you got this because you are grown.
You don't listen to the wise,
As hell caught you by surprise.
You draw weary and faint,
Because your plan you couldn't paint.
He or she said I got you; you believe them but
they ruined you, now what to do?
There was a voice,
That said choose me as your choice.
I can make a way,
And with you stay.
If you trust in me,
Great things I will reveal to thee.
The path I have paved,
And your life I saved.
I always knew the thought,
I was waiting for you so my goodness and glory could be brought.
I have your rewards,
So to me walk towards.
Only I can, man can't do,
Hope, a future, peace, blessings, and life I give to you.
You had to free yourself from yourself and man,
And see the journey of God's plan.

Comes In Threes

God the Father, Jesus the Son, and the Holy Spirit,
Into our lives they fit.
Gold, frankincense, and myrrh,
Gifts to Jesus when His birth occur.
Beginning, middle and end,
A journey to life to send.
The sun, moon, and stars,
To shine light on the dark and heal the scars.
Morning, noon, and night,
To make the day go right.
Father, mother, and child,
The protector, the help meet and nurturer to teach the
offspring so they won't become wild.
Shadrach, Meshach, and Abednego walked thru the fire,
And didn't get burn because trusting God was their desire.
Pray, trust, and wait,
And your blessings, overflow and increase will be great.
Faith, hope and love as love is the greatest of these,
Wonderful things comes in threes.

Will Come Thru

With needed grace,
And mercy to embrace.
When you are about word sink,
He pulls you up without a blink.
When you can't see,
Right there He will be.
It will seem like you going to fall,
He answers to your call.
How you don't know,
Right on time He comes with an overflow.
When things don't seem fine,
His light upon you shines.
When things seem flat,
He will increase that.
As you wonder,
He has already worked it out don't ponder.
He got you,
God will come thru.

What You Say

God uses words as clues,
To get you ready for some good news.
You are about to see something will behold,
As blessings are about to unfold.
Truly it will happen with Verily,
So trust God and watch and see.
With Shall it will manifest,
So prepare for the best.
Think with Selah,
So say thank you, Amen, and Hallelujah.
With Surely it will come to pass,
As you will win, elevate, go to the next level,
and into the next class.
With Ye take heed,
And receive the daily word that God will feed.
When God says your name twice,
He is about to do something in your life because you
were faithful, waited, prayed, and made a sacrifice.
Your miracles are on the way,
Listen carefully, so God what you say?

Choose Purpose Over Pleasure

It's not about material things,
An offering of you to others you need to bring.
God gave life and gives it more abundantly,
His glory, mercy, and grace He wants us to see.
It's for us to have life to enjoy and have fun,
But first His will needs to be done.
Let fulfillment be your plan,
And trust God and not man.
Joy comes from peace,
So the stress of the world release.
Money comes and it goes,
Your gifts and talents use it because if you don't who knows.
Unnecessary things we spend our time on,
But people remember when we touch
them when they were scorned.
Wasted energy and time on a person, thing, or place,
But when you are in your calling you can help,
inspire, reach, encourage, support, and comfort
and that will put a smile on their face.
To love is an ultimate treasure,
So choose purpose over pleasure.

To Stay Number One

You don't have to force anything to take place,
You are destined for this and on you is God's mercy and grace.
It's for you to be on top,
For all you did for others and went through this is just the
beginning because what's for you is coming and it won't stop.
All that you are about to receive you deserve it,
Because you had faith, waited, trusted, and you didn't quit.
The favor on you is heavy,
So for your abundance, overflow, and increase get ready.
There will be so many blessings you won't be able to count solution,
They are coming in double portion, multiplying, adding up,
and in exceeding amounts.
You asked and you shall receive,
Because for it you believe.
You didn't think it could happen for and to you,
Just know miracles and the impossible only God can do.
They will be calling your name,
Because of the God of now, yesterday, today,
forever, and back then is the same.
So praise and thank Him like it's already yours,
This is the year for you that God will pour, open doors,
and give you so much more.
God's will for you is and shall be done,
So know from here on out it's for you to stay number one.

Is The Time Near

For the storms to go away,
And see the impossible and miracles every day.
For the troubles to not last,
And watch God bless me from all I lost in my past.
For the tribulations to cease,
And to finally have happiness and peace.
For the going through to end, and see the results that I mend.
For the trials to be finish,
As my faith will not diminish.
For the problems to have a solution,
As the best, better, and coming out are my intrusion.
For the sufferings to no longer pile,
And after a while to now have a permanent smile.
For the pain to disappear,
And have no more stress, doubts, or fear.
For the hurt to heal, and positive feel.
For the brokenness to be fix,
Now into the live, love, and laugh experience I will mix.
For the lack to stop,
And the favor on my life to pour and to go higher to the top.
That the tests are complete,
As the reaping, abundance, and harvest are my treat.
For the wait to take its course,
And receive and benefit from God the source.
That the negativity and bad will be killed and destroyed
because my winning season is happening this year,
For my overflow, manifest, increase, double
portion, and blessings is the time near?

All Out

Get ready and prepared for the increase,
As blessings God is about to release.
You asking for minimum but God is doing the max,
Because double portion, multiplying, and
exceeding is for you do relax.
You have waited so here comes your time,
So be fruitful and chime.
Into the impossible you have stepped,
As God's promises He has kept.
He is going beyond what you can see,
Your winning season is calling thee.
You will be the proof and evidence of what God can do,
As miracles are all around you.
The unusual, uncommon, unexpected, suddenly,
and surprisingly be ate about to occur,
As the manifest is happening to him and her.
You will be wowed, shocked, numbed, and speechless,
As you in your life how God is about to bless.
So in advance praise Him, thank Him, say God did it, but God,
and the credit give Him all,
Because in new territory, strange places, and in the unfamiliar
and unknown your name will be spoken above and called.
God is going to show you what He's about,
Because for you He is going all out.

We Are In

The now,
As great things God will reveal and allow.
The verily,
So just watch God and see.
The shall,
As God shows us that He is Father, friend, and pal.
The will,
So be faithful and be still.
The behold,
For us the miracles and the impossible will unfold.
Something new,
Get ready for the goodness, exceeding, abundance, overflow,
and increase as there is nothing too hard for God to do.
The manifest,
It's time for us to have the best.
The season to win,
It's beginning what we are in.

To Say

I truly appreciate you,
With the things for me that you do.
You are genuine,
Regardless of where in your life you may have been.
You are a true giver,
And what God has placed on your heart to do, you will deliver.
Your kindness goes a long way,
As you are a blessing to my day.
I'm grateful for your caring gestures,
And creating your smile, calmness, and peace is my pleasure.
Bless you will be,
And it was not by accident but for a reason for you to meet me.
For you I always pray,
Thank you, to you I want to say.

The Wait

Is on God's timetable,
Because His able.
Is for a reason,
As you are entering into your winning season.
Is the test,
Because you will receive the best.
Is for God to reveal,
That the impossible and miracles He will do and that He is real.
Is not a punishment,
Because blessings to you will be sent.
Is for the timing that is right,
And joy, peace, happiness, love, and
perseverance will be your delight.
Is for the good,
And you will be rewarded as you should.
Is to show what God can do,
As God is about to show up and show out for you.
What's for you anticipate,
So know there is a purpose for the wait.

He Hasn't Failed Me Yet

He is right on time always,
He is worth the honor and praise.
He is my support,
And He is my refuge and is always in my court.
He is just a prayer away,
He won't leave me; He is with me to stay.
He is my guide,
In Him I confide.
He fulfills my needs,
I have a roof over my head, a job, clothes
to wear, and me He feeds.
He continues to wake me up every day,
and He answers when I pray.
Whatever I have to face, He gives me grace.
He loves me forever and it is so profound,
and He does not make me frown.
With Him my life is set,
And He hasn't failed me yet.

The Best Is Here

Get prepared for what's in store,
The promises and prayers will be answered for sure.
It's a wonderful feeling that you can't contain,
Because of your faithfulness you will gain.
You waited and have been patient for a long while,
Now God will grant you that permanent smile.
You are walking into something so profound,
As God has turned things around.
Favor, humbleness, and humility got you to this place,
Because you held on to grace.
It's straight ahead,
Because the thoughts, the plans, the hope, and unexpected
Future by God is lead.
It wasn't easy but you trust and believe,
The struggles were real but it's your time to receive.
You prayed for the same every day,
Watch God He is making a way.
It's right in front of you,
The blessings, increase, overflow, and
the abundance unto you due.
It may seem or look faint,
But the perfect picture God has it to paint.
It's there but what are you going to do to claim,
Faith is still a part of the progress so flow in it because
God knows and has already said your name.
Continue to persevere,
Because the best is here.

Miracles

Do you believe,
That something impossible you can retrieve.
It's just like a mustard seed,
Trusting, believing, praying, and having faith are how you feed.
You first have to know that God is real,
And then His power He will reveal.
Others may hear but what you are saying they may doubt,
Because the same God right now is the same God back then
so what He was done and will do you already know about.
You are one,
Because you are still here and Jesus died
for your sins God's only Son.
God said have a relationship with me,
And blessings, healings, overflows and increases you shall see.
It doesn't just happen in the church,
Just look around it happens anywhere so for God search.
It was handed down to you,
So you have the power too.
We all go thru storms, challenges, and obstacles,
But with prayer and faith we can witnesses miracles.

It's Coming

It will be soon,
Your future will be bright like the moon.
What's for you,
Watch what God will do.
In what you trust and believe,
It's your time, your season, and you are ready to receive.
For God to make a way,
The be are happening in any day.
The exception and the attempt,
From God's favor you are not exempt.
What you have been waiting for,
But God is also going to give more.
Just be still and know,
Into your life God will sow,
So hold on and wait,
Trust it's going to be great.
The prayers and ask you constantly keep humming,
Thank you, Jesus, because it's coming.

Keep Pressing

For your destiny to see,
And the person God called you to be.
For higher heights,
And be about faith and not sight.
Until it doesn't tarry anymore,
And don't quit because it's for you to soar.
Because it's for you to win,
Focus on the victory and not where you been.
There is a blessing for your labor,
Because on your life is favor.
Completion choose,
You have nothing to lose.
When things get in your way,
The answer is to pray.
It's for you to push through,
To gain, prosper, make it, and achieve are all you.
Don't stop until it's done.
Trust God because He is the only one.
Easy nothing will ever be,
You have to earn, learn, and yearn to receive
the greater that is waiting for thee.
You have God so no stressing,
And just keep pressing.

A Change

Many blessings God is about to gift,
As in your life it's about to be a shift.
You thinking it can't happen for you,
Trust God the impossible He is about to do.
You are on the top of God's list,
So get ready because what's prepared for you
is a miracle you don't want to miss.
It's going to seem like it's not true,
But your prayers and ask you are about to view.
This is what your life needs,
The breakthrough, overflow, increase, and to manifest
so God is making a way for you indeed.
Things are going to take place that you never thought could be,
But because of your faithfulness, prayers, hope, and wait the
reaping, double portion, multiplying, and rewards you will see.
You deserve it,
So continue to seek God and don't quit.
It's going to show up unexpectedly, suddenly, unusually,
and surprisingly as it will seem strange,
But it's happening for you a change.

Through Christ

Wisdom, knowledge, and common sense play a vital part,
Tapping into it is how success and being fruitful will start.
God is going to bring us from the bottom to the top,
And what's for us will not be able to be touched or stopped.
Let God does His part, we need to do ours,
Nothing happens overnight, so don't let your faith devour.
It's for us to join forces,
And brainstorm and bring together our resources.
When two or more touch and agree,
Things produce and success presents itself and it's because of we.
Things happen when we work together,
It always makes things better.
We make a team,
As it's for us to beam and gleam.
Even two become one,
That's how it's done.
To combine our gifts and talents would be so nice,
Because of who strengthens us we can
do all things through Christ.

Shavetta Craig

We Are Going To Be Smack

Blessings after blessings at our doors and feet will hit,
But there's one thing, we can't faint, draw weary or quit.
It may have been a while,
But God in our lives, He is about to throw a
curve ball and a wow as increase pile.
To the trials, storms, and troubles God is
about to cast a mighty blow,
So we are about to rise up from our low.
Everything is about to become right,
There is no longer a battle because God won the fight.
It's going to come from out of nowhere,
Look at how much for us God cares.
When we look again,
Everything will mend.
So go ahead and get hype,
Because miracles will continue to swipe.
Anything taken, stolen, destroyed, killed, or lost we will get back,
Because with the victory, overflow, harvest, double portion, and
release and manifestation from God we are going to be smack.

Praise Report

Those ask, seek, knock, and prayers are coming through,
There is nothing that our God cannot do.
When we believe,
We shall receive.
The windows of heaven are opened for us,
And it's all because of Jesus.
We spoke it to see,
So access granted and a yes are the answers to thee.
Miracles and the impossible are already in place and on the way,
Look at God showing up and showing out when we pray.
Get ready for the it's done, it shall, it will,
better, soon, and our sigh of relief,
Because of our faith, hope, and belief.
The future will prosper and be bright,
God has already shed on us favor and light.
Hallelujah and thank you we will shout,
Because in God we trust and didn't doubt.
God's timing and will is always in our court,
That's why we are winning and sharing our praise report.

Speak Lord

I need to hear from you,
Please show me what it is for me to do.
To tell me where to go,
And your timing know.
To my heart to create and show love,
And positive thoughts only thinking of.
So I can understand,
And follow your plan.
Of the good,
And keep me covered if you would.
Of your ways,
And let me see brighter days.
To the situation at hand,
As I trust you and not man.
So we can be on one accord,
To my spirit and soul speak Lord.

Off Guard

God is going to work on your behalf,
You will say thank you God and just laugh.
God is going to come through,
Because the impossible is happening for you.
Miracles will come by surprise,
And the unrighteous will be seated and the
righteous will prevail and rise.
What you prayed for will appear,
Because your ask God did hear.
A mighty wind will blow,
Because it's your time to reap from what you sow.
Everything will get into place,
And you will have an abundance of favor and grace.
Things will hit and be different,
As the overflow and increase will be sent.
You will manifest,
And receive the best.
The suffering and storm will cease,
And you will bask in peace.
Everything you wanted will take effect,
Because of your faith and because you are not perfect.
Life and love will be great,
So the experience anticipates.
What's for you is coming and you won't see it,
Your reward because you didn't quit.
I know having faith and trusting God can be hard,
But just know for your faithfulness and waiting
those blessings are going to find you off guard.

Tip Of The Iceberg

God is showing you a preview,
Get excited for how He is about to bless you.
This is just a taste,
Of His everlasting favor and grace.
For what's to come be ready,
It's going to come and continue to flow steady.
God is revealing an inkling,
Of the harvest, double portion, and blessings He is going to bring.
Take heed to the hints and clues,
It is your winning season and you won't lose.
See the glimpse of your possibilities,
Because the wait was worth it to get to your destiny.
God is about to complete the task,
So in the goodness and rewards you will bask.
Receive the downpour,
As in the years to come you will receive more.
This is just the beginning of your release,
As you will see the overflow and increase.
This is the appetizer before the main course,
You will walk into what's for you the resource.
It will be better and great your future to embrace,
As you will be equipped with grace.
Expect it because is it on the arise,
God works suddenly, unexpectedly, on time, and by surprise.
Faith, hope, and love are leading and guiding you,
More than you can ask, think, or imagine God is going to do.
The time has come for the miracles and the impossible to surge,
So this is just the tip of the iceberg.

In Due Season

We shall reap,
Gods promise He will keep.
Good will come back,
And regain what we lack,
We will receive the riches,
The joy, peace, love, and happiness which
are blessings better than wishes.
The miracles we will see,
And better be.
Life will be bright and not dreary,
So we can't quit or become weary.
We will prosper and gain,
And favor on us will sustain.
Do not faint,
Hope and a future God will paint.
Everything happens for a reason,
And what's for us will happen in due season.

God Is Working

In my life I proclaim,
Into my winning season I aim.
My future I will continue to scope,
As I live by faith and rejoice in hope.
Believe even when I don't see,
Because I know it's happening for me.
In the tribulations I will continue to be steadfast,
Because troubles won't last.
In the storms I will be patient because they will pass me by,
Because there will be joy for the tears I cry.
Wait regardless of how it seems,
It's going through the process it will beam.
My prayers have to be consistent,
And for what I ask be persistent.
Constant when I pray,
Because God is making a way.
Be faithful and repetitive,
And I will see the goodness while I live.
Gods timing comes with a price,
So I will be still and know as my ask
and blessings are the sacrifice.
Gods plan for me is being wonderfully orchestrated,
It will be more than I anticipated.
The details for my life He is still twerking,
Even while He is silent God is working.

It's All God

They say one thing,
The impossible to the situation God will bring.
They say you only qualify for this much,
But God shows up and shows out and grants you more than such.
They say this can't be done,
But trust God He has the final say He is the miracle working one.
They say this is not going to go through,
But God provides a way for you.
When man fails,
Then God steps in to prevail.
When they say no,
God says yes, it's a go.
When they say how could this be,
God reveals all power for everyone to see.
When there are faults,
God still comes through to produce great results.
Know your resources faith, trust, belief, prayers, and rod,
Because it shall and will happen for you as it's all God.

Expect, Effort And Endurance

What you ask God for,
And praise Him in advance until it comes
and meets you at your door.
Blessings to flow,
And this too shall pass know.
Better things,
As peace, joy, happiness and love to you God will bring.
The answer to be clear,
As from God you hear.
What's for you find,
It's time to see and not become blind.
In faith you have to step out on,
And follow your destiny for which you were born.
You must give to receive,
And trust, wait and believe.
Always take strive,
And continue to thrive.
It's in you let it peak,
When discovered let it speak.
An answer it expects you to give,
It wants to enter and through you live.
What's for you let it in,
Because it's your season to win.
Be still so from God you can hear,
He reveals Himself in several ways so lend your ear.
When you ask, seek and knock let it be your reassurance,
Because God is on time so He is looking for
your expect, effort, and endurance.

The Good Fight

The punches won't stop,
They try to defeat me and see me drop.
The situation wants me to worry and fret,
But God is bigger and greater as that's what
the enemy wants me to forget.
My finances, habits, flaws, diseases, sicknesses, people,
bitterness, and storms try to hold me down,
In spite of it all I continue to smile when I should frown.
In so many directions there is an attack,
But God, He always have my back.
Stress tries to take me out,
But I'm still here so there is a purpose for me no doubt.
Satan is that all you got,
Because my God is always on time a lot.
Silent prayers may seem unheard,
But God is listening, He said He will never
leave nor forsake you it's in His word.
No matter what they say or do to you,
To yourself and others stay true.
I know it feels like you are on a roller coaster ride,
It's not seen but the blessings God will provide.
God our trust and faith in you let us not lose sight,
Because we will win and overcome in the good fight.

We Are All Sinners

Because of His glory,
We have a story.
Asking for forgiveness is the way,
As God listens when we pray.
Of our sins repent,
And deliverance will be sent.
Saved or not,
God is all we got.
Regardless of your title or who you are mistakes you do make,
So in remembrance of the body broken and the blood shed partake.
We will fall short,
But change is in our court.
Perfect we will never be,
But an effort is what God wants to see.
Life will have distractions and temptations come our way,
So let hope, faith, mercy, and grace guide us each day.
We won't always do what's right,
But of our purpose and assignment let's not lose sight.
From Jesus a sacrifice was paid,
For every sin we will do and already made.
Even with the bad habits that are hard to kill,
God can deliver just trust Him and be still.
Little or big all sins are seen the same as one,
Just know that God's will shall be done.
Simply and complex sins we do commit,
But our lives to Jesus we should submit.
It's for us to be winners,
Regardless if we are all sinners.

Access Granted

This is for you,
God said come through.
The storms, trials and tribulations are not going to take you out,
Blessings on blessings are what you are going to be about.
God is able,
So have a seat at His table.
By faith you invest,
Now walk into it your best.
The prayers were heard,
What you asked for will be given it's God's word.
It's your time to enter in,
It's for you to win.
All you have to do is say,
And God's command is on the way.
God didn't forget about you,
Everything He say He is about to do.
Troubles won't last,
Just like that miracles will shower down and on you cast.
It's been said and done,
Open the doors and receive said the ultimate One.
For the tarry of the mustard seeds planted,
The wait is over because access granted.

Shavetta Craig

Double Portion

By faith I will live,
My all to you God I will give.
Where my ancestors and loved ones left off,
I will carry on,
Regardless of the pain,
be hurt and scorn.
To me God add,
And day by day progress I will show and be glad.
When I ask, seek, and knock,
I know you hear me, so though it tarry,
I will wait because my blessings you won't block.
As favor is my increase,
In my life there will be an overflow release.
I will continue to pray,
And in your will stay.
Walking in my winning season,
As trusting you is the reason.
Your mercy, grace, glory, and power are my notion,
So God please grant me a double portion.

Wait For It

It may seem like it is taking so long,
What was promised will be given just remain strong.
The ask was heard,
Just stay grounded on Jesus' word.
It will tarry,
But your faith continues to carry.
Everything about you will be tested,
And when you least expect it that's when the
blessings will come in which you invested.
Patience is something you have to learn,
And in your endurance, you will receive everything you yearn.
Give it the time to grow what you planted,
And in due season the harvest will be granted.
Time is a precious thing,
Its arrival is so perfect greatness it brings.
Suddenly you will see,
The overflow, like a flood, catches you by surprise
and like a ram in the bush for thee.
So do life day by day,
And continue to trust and pray.
The wealth, health, love, happiness, peace, goodness, favor,
and joy will be yours in heaven and on earth,
But first a testimony, story, process, storms, tribulations,
failures, and pain will be on this journey that is birth.
It will not come easy now or ever just don't quit,
Because it will happen at the appointed hour so wait for it.

Shavetta Craig

Like A Stain

Come in,
And cleanse my sins.
I need you to stay,
As I thank you every day.
In my soul leave a permanent mark,
And let always love from my heart spark.
You from my head to my feet,
Favor and touch me and next to me take a sit.
You are all I got,
So in my spirit pick a spot.
Please in me never come out,
Because your guidance I'm all about.
Always with me remain,
And dwell in this vessel like a stain.

Release And Manifestation

It was heard and spoken,
The promises, impossible, and miracles will be woken.
What was prayed about and asked for will be dispatched,
And the favor of God is on you attached.
An overflow will drop,
And debts and lacks will stop.
The promise to keep,
And blessings to reap.
It will show and not hide,
God's timing has come, so now He will provide.
On you God will blow, spiritually, physically, mentally, and
emotionally, socially, and most of all financially you will grow.
This year is just the beginning,
The season of winnings.
The increase has your name on it, Because you didn't quit.
Trusting, believing, and waiting are going to pay off for you,
Just watch and see what God will do.
Just like a present,
Here is your gift unwrap it greatness is inside for you it's meant.
The mustard seeds are going to produce,
Elevation to you will be introduce.
You planted and watered but you thought it will tarry
no; it's your time to sow, flourishing you will know.
What God said will be granted unto you,
You ask, seek, and knock for it, so here it is your breakthrough.
God is about to exceed your expectations,
Because it's in the atmosphere the year
of release and manifestation.

Shavetta Craig

In The Mess

They have done you bad,
And for that you are hurt and mad.
To you they were not fair,
With the many years given and dedication they don't care.
It caught you by surprise,
But they have shown you many signs of
deceit that it opened your eyes.
You cried, questioned, got angry and got your pressure high,
Let it go so to that job say goodbye.
God has removed you from the hell,
From this a blessing you will be able to tell.
Right or wrong,
You just continue to remain strong.
Now it's to cloudy to see,
But the reason will reveal itself to thee.
You are not on the bottom because you are on the top,
Because what God has for you no job or man can stop.
Don't get discouraged or feel low,
God has you this I know.
Gods favor is still on you,
As something bigger and better in your life He will do.
Wait and see God will bless,
Even in the mess.

Gods Will Be Done

Praying is the key,
As God says trust and wait on me.
Suddenly there is a happening of things,
As we ask God for healing and deliverance to bring.
Things seems to be going fine then it turns for the worse,
God, please break and cast away the cancer, COVID,
diseases, illnesses, and sicknesses curse.
God you are the only source to come to,
It's in your hands so do what you have the power to do.
The pain and hurt are hard to endure,
God your strength, power, mercy, and grace we need for sure.
By your word we will stand,
As we rely on you and not man.
You said you wouldn't put too much on us to bear,
So God of this situation take care.
We don't like to see our loved ones suffer like this,
So the agony, fear, tears, and burdens dismiss.
We pray and give it to you,
Your healing touch and purpose do.
Continue to have faith and trust in the Father,
Holy Spirit, and Son,
As God's will be done.

I Will Trust

In my storm,
Believing that blessings and miracles will form.
When I can't see,
Faith will have to be the guide for me.
When I don't see a way,
All I know to do is pray.
When the situation is oblique,
God I will continue to seek.
When doubt comes,
I have to know where my help comes from.
When I continue to be faced with troubles,
My time will come to receive double.
When my own burdens I get myself into,
Here comes God to carry me thru.
When it seems like good and a way out is
never going to happen for me,
Without quitting a breakthrough will be.
I fall get back up and again fall,
I have to keep going and give God and myself my all.
I make progress but I keep getting knocked down,
I have to continue to press until God turns things around.
To have a better life and being is a must,
So in God I will trust.

The Power Of Prayer

It's an important part of your day,
And it will make a way.
Continue to do it constantly,
So results you can see.
God's timing is everything,
The answer, solution, and blessings to you He will bring.
Count on it,
Trust, have faith, believe, and wait just don't quit.
Patience and endurance are the key,
And let the spirit lead thee.
It's the most important ingredient,
And it's been proven to work when you are obedient.
What you speak,
A move from God will peak.
God is always there,
In the power of prayer.

Delayed But Not Denied

I'm still waiting,
Gods timing I'm anticipating.
The timing may seem paused,
It will happen right on time at all cause.
Wait for it,
Just don't quit.
It may have a halt,
It's coming it's not your fault.
It will take its time and creep,
When you least expect it, you will reap.
The process is slow,
It will happen for you just know.
It will make you think it's not on the way,
It's unseen it will happen one day.
Be still and hush,
What God is doing don't rush.
It may seem like it's not happening for you,
To your faith and purpose stay true.
Patience you tried,
Just wait on the Lord because it's delayed not denied.

Jesus, I Love You

I thank you every day,
As several times to you I pray.
You are my guard,
And you are there when things get hard.
You give me hope,
When with life I can't cope.
A way you always make,
When I want to give up and break.
You give me the wisdom to see,
That there is greater inside of me.
Every time you provide,
And my life you guide.
You give me a reason to live,
As my life to you I give.
Your timing is always right,
That's why on you I won't lose sight.
Blessings you reveal,
And you answer prayers and heals.
You give me love and peace,
As your spirit and power, you release.
I don't deserve what you do,
Jesus, I love you.

God Is Working In Your Favor

When it's hard meeting ends meet,
God always made things complete.
When you are standing there in court,
Any verdict He can abort.
No need to worry, He will see you thru and tell your story.
When it looks grey,
To Him pray.
You don't have to run,
It's worked out and done.
While being in that hospital bed,
By a mighty healer you are led.
When it doesn't look right,
To the situation He brings light.
When you didn't know what road to take,
God held your hand to guide you on the path to take,
You He never forsakes.
When your bills exceed your income,
God always worked it out even though you didn't
know where the blessings came from.
As you scrap and scrape,
God allowed for you an escape.
When you couldn't see,
He already took care of it for thee.
Through the struggle, humble, and stumbles,
He wants you to trust in Him and remain humble.
He is always with you; He is your breakthrough.
Go ahead and tell your neighbor,
That God is working in your favor.

I Don't Deserve

Your timing that is always right,
And thru my darkness you shed and shine your light.
You blessing me,
And the favor that I have and a way out to see.
The love that you give,
And the life I live.
All that you do,
And the things I have that are because of you.
Your mercy and grace,
Because of my own sins I embrace.
Your strength and power,
As in wrongdoing I devour.
For you to catch me when I fall,
Because I'm not perfect at all.
The sacrifices you have done,
Or to be called you daughter or son.
And for me not to serve, thank or be grateful to you what nerve,
What you have added unto me I don't deserve.

Let It Harvest

Bring forth good fruits,
And happiness as the pursuit.
Rise from the old,
And walk the path of greatness to behold.
To see marvelous things,
And what's in stored for you the Lord will bring.
Being excited for the few,
As a result of abundance for the new.
Amazing each day will be,
With miracles to see.
Blessings will be like a downpour,
And favor happening more and more.
Prayers will be answered in the right timeline,
And right on time things will work out fine.
The gifts in you to produce,
As to your timing you are introduced.
Love will blossom again and thrive,
As rekindling and reconciling will keep it alive.
Dreams, goals, business, and change will sprout,
Winning we are doing with no doubt.
We have stepped into our best,
So let it harvest.

The Un Experience

Unexpected things will happen for you,
Your hope and future you will view.
Unexplainable miracles will take place,
And the time has come for you to win and favor embrace.
Unpredictable God will and can be,
But what He can do you will see.
Unstoppable will be the overflow, increase, and blessings,
It's happening so no stressing.
Unspeakable the joy, peace, love, and happiness will occur,
It will sneak up on you, slap you in the face,
and appear so quickly that it will be like a blur.
Uncomfortable God has to make you,
So the impossible and what you deserve He can do.
Uncontainable will be the harvest, double
portion, multiplying, and rewards,
So to God's plan and will keep walking towards.
Just know that underline in timing will all make sense,
And welcome the un experience.

Stop Worrying

I'm about to bless you above measure,
And they will see your treasures.
Your Eros love will find you,
And what you asked for I will do.
Better days are on the way,
And know I hear you when you pray.
It will happen when the time is right,
Just be still and know I got you because
your battles for you I will fight.
This too shall pass,
Because storms, troubles, and problems won't always last.
Your tears will dry,
Because you didn't give up or quit, you always try.
You will love, be happy, and have peace again,
And you will mend.
Your talents and gifts will manifest and birth,
And everyone will know your worth.
Everything is going to work out,
So don't fear or doubt.
About tomorrow,
And dwell in joy and not sorrow.
About the challenges and the things that you go
through that are occurring,
This is God, I got you so stop worrying.

I May Not Understand

What God is up to,
But God, I trust you.
When it's going to happen for me,
But God, He will reveal it at the appointed time for me to see.
The plan and details,
God did it and He's doing it and He will prevail.
But it's working out for my good,
And everything will happen when it should.
The reason for the why,
But when I see the manifestation, it will
make sense and tears of joy I will cry.
The wait,
But I do know with God in the midst it's going to be great.
The storms, troubles, trials, tribulations, sufferings, and falls,
But in God's timing my setup is my comeback to reap back all.
God had it orchestrated and prepared for me and He has my hand,
Even when I may not understand.

It's Working Out

Hold on and just don't let go,
Because you are about to receive your overflow.
Your situation is about to turn around,
So hold your head up high and straighten your crown.
The wait is just a part of the process,
Just watch and see you are about to be bless.
Don't let God silence fool you,
Because the impossible in your life He is about to do.
For what's coming make room because
God is going to make a way,
He is providing to everything that you asked for when you pray.
You have come too far to fail,
So be attentive because the miracles in your life will prevail.
your faith, hope, and trust are getting you somewhere,
Because for you God cares.
You remained faithful, humble, thankful,
and grateful even when it was hard to,
It's your time and season to come through.
You were being prepared for this,
Your opportunity you won't miss.
Don't look at your storm, trouble, and suffering as a bad thing,
Look forward at the reward and harvest God is about to bring.
Now is not the time to break or doubt,
Because everything in your favor it's working out.

Giants Do Fall

Whatever you face,
Have the faith to embrace.
Troubles come and go,
Because it's for you to win and conquer this I know.
Whatever comes at you please believe you will defeat,
As the favor on your live is on repeat.
Before you that situation may stand,
But trust that there is power in your hands.
You are equipped for this,
So the problem will dismiss.
No storm will stand in your way,
Because there is power when you pray.
Remain faithful and humble,
As what presents itself before you will crumble.
No matter how big or strong,
Just know it won't last long.
So don't be afraid,
Because it will lose and away fade.
What was lost, taken, or destroyed you will get back all,
Because giants do fall.

Wait For It

Joy will be everlasting,
And great things on you are casting.
Peace you will endure,
And grace will be with you for sure.
Happiness you will have for a lifetime,
And your heart again will chime.
Love will last and sustain,
And forever remain.
Hope that will be for an eternity,
And the goodness that will follow thee.
The destiny, dreams, desires, and the great future that is near,
Continue to have faith and persevere.
A gem you are,
As your winning season is not far.
God is working it out for your good,
So it can happen as it should.
Get excited again,
What's for you is coming my friend.
Your time will come and the fire will be lit,
Patience is worth the virtue so wait for it.

Before It Happens

Get in position,
As things transition.
Know it will be,
Even when you can't see.
Trust the preparation and process,
Because you are going to be bless.
Thank God in advance,
For the favor, the victory, the breakthrough,
the miracle, the impossible, and another chance.
Continue to pray,
Because what's for you is on the way.
Believe, be still, and know,
Because what God can do,
He is going to show.
Be ready,
Because unexpectedly and suddenly that wind will blow steady
Have faith, hope, and laughter,
And continue to praise Him after.
Claim, declare, decree, receive, and wait as the door opens,
So do this before it happens.

Shavetta Craig

The Turn Around

Be still and know,
For something great to happen the process will be slow.
Just continue to pray,
And in faith stay.
Trust in God always,
And now before it happens give Him glory and praise.
Waiting you must do,
Because God is going to come through.
Gods timing is never known,
But what He has for you, right on time it will be shown.
Unexpectedly God will do,
Just know it's happening for you.
As suddenly something can change and be,
What's for you prepare for it because God's favor you will see.
What's about to happen for you will be so profound,
So get ready for the turn around.

I Will Trust You

With the things done to me and my own mistakes,
Forgive and be forgiven and you will correct
it because you won't forsake.
With my life's plan,
If anyone can do it you can.
To provide,
And to stay by my side.
To change things all around,
And listen for your voice the sound.
To order my steps,
And your promises kept.
To see me to the end,
And love unconditional send.
To heal what is broken,
And believe in your words that were spoken.
With the journey to see your light,
As things in my life get right.
To change the people and loved ones that I care for,
And of you give them more.
To let the bad and past fade,
As a beautiful new beginning is made.
Man can't do,
Lord, I will trust you.

Shavetta Craig

When We Go Through

Difficulties, problems, troubles, and our cry,
It's like a storm that will pass on by.
It won't last always,
Through it still give God the praise.
Pain and suffering in some type of way we all will endure,
But the blessings and rewards will come for sure.
In that predicament it's not for us to stay,
That's why we have to always pray.
Believe you will come out,
And block the fears and doubts.
Our faith is tested,
And how much time with God we invested.
Easy is not the way,
Hard work, sacrifices, and your all must come into play.
The requirement is God, trusting you,
So go to God when we go through.

Remain Silent

In faith be,
Because in any moment now your blessings you will see.
Don't change or become different,
Continue to act normal and be resilient.
How God blesses you others don't need to know,
Just let the goodness of God on you show.
So continue to pray, trust, and wait,
And your release, manifestation, overflow, financial
freedom, increase, and favor anticipate.
Let wisdom be your guide,
And watch God provide.
This is a you and God thing,
As the desires of your heart, He bring.
You will reap back from the lost, stolen, pain, hurt, robbery,
and the many times you cried and bled,
So in your secret place thread.
Your gratitude and humbleness will carry you a long way,
Because something amazing, big, mind blowing,
and unexpected are about to happen in any day.
When what God has for you is sent,
Thank Him, smile, and remain silent.

The Comeback

It's going to be real,
It I can feel.
I may have been knocked down,
But I'm getting back up to receive something so profound.
On this journey I have been through a lot for sure,
But there is a blessing for me to endure.
For the hell and not so easy assignments that I went
through there is something great for me to see,
The winnings, favor, and overflow are all on me.
The storms, struggles, troubles, and tests
are about to come to an end,
And I will reap and be prepared and equipped if it happens again.
Failures can't hold me down,
Success will find me and I will wear my crown.
The enemy thought he had me, thinking he was clever,
He forgot who I belong to, so enemy I won but you never.
The big is after me,
It's waiting for me to receive what I'm about to see.
I'm about to reap from every stab, brokenness,
hurt, pain, regrets, bleed, and lack,
As I'm ready and God is preparing me for the comeback.

A Re

What's in the way or a hinderance will be removed,
And what's for you it will replace and that God will prove.
God will erase your past and do a rewind,
And this time He will do it; He replay and it
will be right and it will blow your mind.
He will reveal everything to you at the appointed time,
As he restores you and your heart again will chime.
He will refresh you,
And remind you what He can do.
He will reset and restart,
So rejoice now while He does His part.
Receiving be prepared for,
Because the revelation is for you to have above
all you can ask or think and even more.
He will give you a reason for a sigh of relief,
As He rewards you because of your faith belief.
Your request He heard,
As you relied on His word.
Ask and it will be retrieved back to you,
And watch the release, manifestation,
and reaping you will view.
Repent, refocus, and repair over and over again,
As a redo is always welcomed and make reaching a trend.
The resolution which are the miracles
and impossible for you to see,
As God do for you are.

When We Don't Deserve It

His grace,
But He continues to see us through anything that we face.
His mercy as a refuge,
No matter what we do His love for us is always huge.
His forgiveness,
He still forgives even though we caused the mess.
His blessings over our life,
As we still judge, envy, and have strife.
His glory,
Because we lack faith and still fear and worry.
His hands and blood on us,
As we still continue to hate, fight and fuss.
What we do have,
As the enemy sees how bless and fortunate we are at us he laughs.
His favor that He provides,
As doing wrong and right in our lives collides.
We sin, fall short, deny, and take a break from God but
on us He will never quit,
He will always have us even when we don't deserve it.

The Choice Is Yours

By faith we need to walk,
Show action and less talk.
It was spoken over my life,
A change of scenery is going to break me free from the strife.
Fears and doubts you will have to put aside,
We just have to know that God will provide.
We can't miss out on this breakthrough,
As the spirit I will follow and the flesh and
current situation I won't view.
It's not for us to stay,
So get ready, set, and go all the way.
To God's plan we have to stick,
So the distractions and the negativity we must knick.
It's not the time to be or act confuse,
A God is revealing thru another hints and clues.
God is waiting on us for Him to open doors,
So will you stay or leave the choice is yours.

Don't Lose

The ability to hope,
So don't quit continue to cope.
You, in your storm,
Something better will form.
The determination to conquer and win,
Just use your gifts and talents within.
The passion to see an opportunity come true,
Because it's in you.
Sight of what can be,
So that business, house, plan, spouse, and future see.
The power to dream,
And that it's for you to gleam.
Out because you couldn't wait,
Patience rewards you with something great.
Your mind overthinking,
And in misery don't be sinking.
So your drive, success, elevation,
and strength choose,
And your faith in God don't lose.

He Will

Offer and give so much more,
And for me provide for.
Come right on time,
And make my heart chime.
Be the peace that I need,
And will only know the meaning of healing
and not causing any bleed.
Love unconditionally as he should,
And to me always be good.
Give me an experience to endure,
And keep me happy for sure.
Be my answered prayer,
And provide the much-needed care.
Pray for and with me,
And my worth and virtue see.
Put me as a priority,
And put God first his authority.
See me as a gem and treasure to his life,
And make me his best friend and one day his wife.
Be my everything,
And what's needed in my life he will bring.
What's necessary and missing he will have,
And make sure that I live, love, and laugh.
God is in control so he is going to fit the bill,
So to be for me, he will.

God Is, Not Me

In control,
As He is needed to my soul.
The one who can do,
All the credit, honor, praise, glory,
and thank you to Him is due.
Who will make a way,
And wakes me up every day.
The first and last,
And sees me through my past.
The reason for my blessings,
It's me the one stressing.
The pilot, navigation, chief, and conductor,
And the one to have a plan, provide, and
give instructions as the instructor.
To make things happen is all Him,
He is the light to my dim.
For the miracles and impossible to see,
God is, not me.

Leave It

It's for you to go through,
But the figuring out and solving is not up to you.
To God when you make it known and plain,
Let it with Him remain.
Don't give it to Him and then try to take it back,
That's why and how the enemy is after you to attack.
Your children, family, friends, finances, career, life,
problems, and storms put it at God's feet,
So let God's will be done and He will complete.
So trust God and in faith go,
When the time is right,
He will let you know.
Go on with your day, be still, pray, and wait,
And for your victory just anticipate.
It's not for you to stress, doubt, or worry,
Just know that God is about to give you a new story.
When you say God I put it in your hands,
Do just that and let Him do what He does,
so don't worry about the when, how,
or why it's not for you to understand.
Your assignment is to trust God and don't quit,
So everything that you are going through with God leave it.

I'm In The Season of

What's next to reveal,
God is going to show me that He is real.
Recovering all my lacks,
God will give it right back.
A refill,
God is about to pour back into me so I must be still.
Getting replenished,
Because with me God is not finish.
Yet to receive,
So many blessings for me to retrieve.
The reaping,
Because God's promises His keeping.
Manifesting rewards,
As by faith I'm walking towards.
Winning on repeat,
It will keep happening for me as the abundance I will meet.
My release,
Because what's for me will bring me peace.
Just because and for no reason miracles will resurface,
And will happen on purpose.
Reassuring me,
That the impossible I will see.
Rejoicing now for the later,
Because it's going to be greater.
Restoring, regaining, and renewing love,
I'm ready because I'm in the season of.

Where Is Your Faith

It's about believing in the for,
To receive so much more.
Your hope must be involved,
For the blessings to revolve.
In what you see, is what you get is not true,
Because it's the unseen that God is preparing for you.
It's evidence,
That is not yet in your presence.
If you say God is able,
Then trust Him with everything going on in your life
to provide even with putting food on your table.
Don't get caught up in the now,
What's to come, shall, and what will be allow.
The present don't seek,
It's the beyond and future for you to peek.
You have to use your spiritual eyes,
Because it manifests by surprise.
It's that substance for you to anticipate,
That's why it's for you to pray, trust, and wait.
The new beginnings start in the eighth,
So where is your faith?

Let Us Not See

The bank account balance getting low,
God said that He is God, so be still and know.
The credit cards being used more and debit becoming high,
On God rely.
The lifestyle of robbing Peter to pay Paul,
Have faith, hope, and love it's going to take all.
The situations we are in,
Because it's for us to win.
This is not the view and purpose for you,
Just don't quit God is going to see us through.
What the enemy is doing,
Because with us God is plucking, pruning, plunging,
picking, prepping, positioning, promoting, and
preparing us for the blessings to be pursuing.
The physical,
We have to seek the spiritual.
Believe that the overflow and abundance will and shall be,
So with what's happening now, let us not see.

An Empty Cup

Creating me new,
God my life belongs to you.
I know and see now that you are a need,
So God saturate me like a bleed.
In the greater, best, better, and the good I believe,
As from you God I want to receive.
I have plenty of space,
So increase me with your glory, mercy, endurance,
favor, discernment, spirit, and grace.
I made room so I am shallow,
So pour into me until I overflow.
No longer with my flesh I want to wrestle,
So here I am for you an available vessel.
I have a dwelling place to withhold and
absorb what you have to give,
My life with you God I want to live.
God fill me up,
As I am to you an empty cup.

Instant

God is always on time, He is never late,
No matter how long you have to wait.
It just takes His touch,
What is needed so much.
Never stop, always move,
And only at the appointed hour the impossible
God will prove.
Your faith will manifest a shift,
And the blessings will be swift.
Everything is not going to happen snappy,
Just trust God because when it does you will be happy.
Your miracles are on express,
Because it's for you to be bless.
It wasn't a delay or punishment it was
to prepare you for the sudden,
Because this is the season for you to win.
Just when you think it's not happening
immediately God intercepts,
Your prayers, tears, and hope are the rapid concept.
When you continue to flow with no resistant,
God will do what needs to be done in an instant.

Believe It

That your winning season is near,
And have courage and not fear.
Faith is what going to get you through,
So what's meant for you view.
That the tears will stop,
And joy, happiness and peace in your life will drop.
That the troubles will end,
And from anything you can mend.
Miracles will happen in any day,
And blessings are on the way.
The debts, the court case, the bad report, negative
bank account and stress will be dismiss,
But God got this.
The doubts will fade,
Because a way God has made.
What you asked God for,
If you trust Him,
He will give you that and more.
That everything you go through know there is a reward,
Your breakthrough won't be easy but continue to press towards.
What you lost better you will receive back,
And your life will get back on track.
The key is not to quit,
What's for you will come just believe it.

It's About Being A Blessing

When they least expect,
You do something nice from something not perfect.
We wonder from time to time how the bad reap,
And those that struggle stress more than they sleep.
Unforeseen things find you for a reason,
Just make sure you are helping another in each season.
Don't look at it as a take,
Move right along and with others bread break.
Hovered by favor and so many prayers,
You don't get caught because you give back by
showing so many that you care.
Your conscious plays a big part too,
God forgives and forgets; He will always see you through.
No, it wasn't earned or yours,
But by grace it saved you and others by
making a way thru many doors.
Repent and keep peace,
And grasp the blessings, impossible and options as they release.
Bad or good is not for stressing,
So don't just think about you, also it's about being a blessing.

Overflow Me

You said it can be done,
Count me in as one.
Your will can give us our desires,
As blessings starts to inspire.
With a prayer say,
And watch and wait for unexpected things
to happen for you any day.
My heart Lord you know,
As in every aspect of my life you will have me to grow.
What it looks like now it will not stay,
I will receive from my pause, halt, stop and delay.
Faithful and humbleness will have me to win,
And I will never have to go back to that
dark and miserable place I've been.
My life will not be the same,
Miracles will take place in Jesus' name.
The Lord's promises He will keep,
Because I'm destined to reap.
Speak it and it shall be,
Lord, please overflow me.

Be Mindful And Watchful

A wolf betraying to be a sheep,
And a promise they can't keep.
Smile in your face,
But eventually causes disgrace.
Sells you a dream,
And backs down and say there is no I in team.
There true identity is expose,
Who would have thought no one knows.
They say they have a heart of gold,
But a dragged in your back they hold.
Their favorite line is,
I got you,
And then say I'm sorry there is nothing I can do.
It turns out they are a hot mess,
Causing all kinds of problems, drama, and stress.
They display open arms and being giving,
But in selfishness they are living.
To love you partake,
To trust them you have made the biggest mistake.
They turned out to be dark and dull,
Of people please be mindful and watchful.

Stop Running

Fears you must face,
Trust and have faith because God is trying
to put you in the right place.
Risks you will always have to take in life,
As success begins when you let go of the past and of your strife.
Doubts leave them behind,
So be at peace and free your mind.
For your situation to change,
You have to become uncomfortable and see things
start happening even when it's strange.
Listen to God and not you,
Something better for your life God wants you to view.
It's for you to take in the unfamiliar,
And reach for goals, dreams, and winnings nothing particular.
Put your heart and mind to it and go,
Don't second guess and no excuses so better for you know.
It's for you to achieve,
So conceive, believe, and receive.
It's time for you to be stunning,
So embrace your blessings and stop running.

I Will Pass The Test

Challenges keep coming for me,
But I will keep my faith because my blessings I will see.
My strength they continue to try,
But I will see joy and happiness from the tears I cry.
Something bad seems to happen every day,
But I believe in God to make a way.
Not getting back what I give,
Thank God it's for Him I live.
Words, attitudes, messiness, and bitterness at me you throw,
But I will still kill you with kindness this I know.
You want to break me down,
I won't let you I will stand my ground.
When the next is not being fair,
I still give a care.
When about me they talk,
I will hold my head high and with determination walk.
Frustration wants to defeat,
But peace will make me complete.
Whatever comes my way I will get through it and receive the best,
Because I will pass the test.

Destine For A Destiny

It's for you to be great,
And it's fate.
As you search,
When you least expect it, your purpose will perch.
The calling on your life was given since you were a child,
It's time to listen you already did your share of being wild.
In you all possibilities fill,
But God is waiting for you to be still.
So with your life you can know what to do,
Stop running because God is waiting on you.
Your name was given and it fits,
It wants to reveal to you so get in a secret place and sit.
Listen clear,
So from God you can hear.
Draw your attention close,
And the knowledge and wisdom absorb every dose.
You had your fun,
What you are suppose to be doing in life
make room for it and get it done.
The good, bad and the ugly you had your share of plenty,
So make space because you are destine for a destiny.

Live By

The Lord will come through,
In His timing He will rescue you.
Don't go by how it appears,
Just have faith with no fears.
Life can give you a scare,
But there is a higher power so beware.
When answers you seek,
Just wait for God to speak.
Keep saying it and believing unto you see,
Regardless of how long it will happen for thee.
The talk,
And by faith walk.
Miracles and the impossible happens every day,
That's why it's so very important to pray.
Results and blessings will produce,
Our God has no excuse.
I tell you no lie,
The power of prayer live by.

It's Going To Be Big

For the tears you cry,
And how you continue to try.
Even with the challenges and struggles you have been thru,
And when you wanted to giving up and quitting you didn't do.
You continue to wait without seeing a thing,
Patiently on God you wait for the blessings
and promises He will bring.
The bad things said,
And having sleepless nights in your bed.
For doing your all,
And others doing things to see you uncomfortable and
wanting to see you fall.
People doing things to you intentionally,
But this too shall pass watch and see.
For your stress,
And you will make it to your success.
Being mistreated, used, and talked about,
God sees don't doubt.
Without seeing results, you continue to be still,
Keep your faith it's God's will.
Your trust in God rely,
As timing is everything and watch the
increase and overflow multiply.
You are going to be fruitful like a fig,
Because for all you been thru your blessings it's going to be big.

Worth The Wait

Your timing,
As everything in my life will be chiming.
The process,
Even though it takes time it's for me to be bless.
Your blessings,
So there is no need for me to be stressing.
What you have in store,
Because you will give more.
The win,
As something new will begin.
Who you are preparing for me,
And the amazing future I will see.
Your plan,
And doing the miracles and the impossible only you can.
What you have plan God I will anticipate,
Because what you have for me is worth the wait.

Breath And Live

From darkness you suffocate,
Open up and let light create.
Your secrets are cutting off your oxygen flow,
So communicate and let it go.
With your grudges and bad memories,
you are holding on for dear life,
Now is the time to free yourself from your strife.
Being haunted by your past keeps you grasping for air,
Cut your ties from them and get the help to repair.
Your bad thoughts and habits are stopping your air supply,
So on change rely.
To get off life support you have to dismiss the mess,
And breath again without the distractions and stress.
Get rid of bad oxygen,
And inhale where you are going and exhale where you have been.
When you remove emotions, hurt, guilt, fear, doubts,
and pain then of yourself you can give,
So breath and live.

Don't Look At It As A Setback

Mistakes you made,
And a hefty price you paid.
The storms and tribulations continue to stack,
It's your strength to give you wisdom to get you on track.
You slipped and fell,
And even had to be rescued from hell.
It's like you keep trying and you can't seem to get it,
But the keys are patience, waiting and don't quit.
Don't get discouraged just continue to forward move,
And what's for you God will prove.
No one is perfect,
But an error, misjudgment and wrong choices can be corrected.
Your decisions may not always be great,
But a solution you can create.
Just because something you wanted and had was snatched,
You have what it takes to start again from scratch.
It's about getting back up and keep going,
And improvements keep showing.
Things in your life you may lack,
But get ready for your comeback and don't look at it as a setback.

I Want

What God has for me,
And His plan for my life to unfold so I can see.
His will,
So that means I have to wait on Him and be still.
The grace that He gives,
And in my life this vessel I need Him to dwell and live.
His favor,
And to be led by my Savior.
Your love everlasting,
Having you is the best thing asking.
Greatness to always follow,
And continue to have strength and endurance tomorrow.
Happiness to be my definition,
And being humble, faithful, grateful, and
thankful each day a repetition.
Light to make me shine,
And anything that tries to come up against
me God says I got this you are fine.
What God has placed in me to be contagious,
As my reflection blesses and changes other and be outrageous.
Peace forevermore,
And blessings to always greet me at my door.
To in faith step,
And for my future prep.
To have patience and don't let worry and fear taunt,
Whatever you have for me God is what I want.

Perfect What Or Who

It's for God in us to prevail,
Because we will fail.
We won't always do everything right,
But of the source don't lose sight.
We will fall,
Just know who to call.
We can be blind,
But we can again see and have a renewed mind.
We don't always play our hands straight,
We serve a God that cleanse, forgive, forget, and is great.
The world is filled with temptation,
Stay prayed up and let Jesus be your sensation.
We will come short,
But on Jesus don't abort.
In Jesus believe,
Because sometimes we can deceive.
There will always be room for improvement and change in you,
Because God and His Son Jesus are the only perfect what or who.

Use Your Wings And Fly

Fear shouldn't get in your way,
Step out of your comfort zone, soar, and pray.
On faith and in you rely,
Because joy is coming for the tears you cry.
Get yourself in a position to conquer,
And as you change then you will see
great things around you occur.
Watch, listen and you will see,
The plan awaits you so better you can be.
Don't let doubt and negative thoughts and people hold you back,
Know who you are and your destiny face stay on track.
You have been in the same place too long,
Opportunities and growth see you, so it's
time for you to become strong.
Failures and mistakes you have been thru,
But it was to discover what is truly in you.
Take the effort, determination and try,
It's been given to you so use your wings and fly.

Open Doors

You can't go back in once it's shut,
Seek other opportunities from your rut.
There will be many or a few,
Let God led you to the one that is for you.
Your talents should be your drive,
To your destiny strive.
God has doors closed and open for a reason,
Take heed to God's voice in this season.
Don't be afraid to approach,
Let faith and hope be your guide coach.
It's no time to be timid so be bold,
Because there is something great for you to behold.
You stayed behind one door too long,
There are other places and other doors you
need to be at so don't prolong.
For you blessings pours,
Because God has created for you open doors.

Weather The Storms

Challenges and struggles you will endure,
But continue to believe in Jesus as He will guide you for sure.
You are equipped with power and strength
to get thru it and make it cease,
Because Jesus is Lord of peace.
Don't wrestle, fight, draw weary or faint not just be still,
Jesus will do His will.
Storms come to see if you have faith in God's word,
And if you are believing, trusting and taking heed to what
He has promised you that you have read and have heard.
Each storm has a different duration,
Just stand strong, embrace and conquer it and know
it too shall pass and have an expiration.
Storms are to build you,
With all power, endurance, strength, faith,
and might to do God's will you can do.
Storms are the training,
To keep you fit, focus, refresh, aware, and ready for your gaining.
Storms will come and go,
So be prepared to speak to it and your victory know.

Storms has its reasons,
So that's your sign for a shift, turnaround, change, push,
increase, elevation, and a blessing in disguise in that season.
Remember to remain and stay humble,
Don't let any storm make you crumble.
Just know that God has you,
And He will see you thru.
No matter how big or small,
The storm will bow down to you and cease and fall.
Just know greatness, new growth, a new image,
elevation, and deliverance will form,
When you weather your storms.

Don't Let Your Past Predict Your Future

I know you expected a forever and lifetime,
But you were broken and dropped like a dime.
This is not what you wanted for your life,
But you believed in, trusted, loved, and gave your
all to that unfaithful husband or wife.
Your world and heart they hurt,
You felt like dirt.
From all you gave and done,
You couldn't believe that you were deceived by
that person that you thought was the one.
All the energy and time you put in,
They followed after lust, flesh, temptation, and sin.
From hurt, pain, brokenness, and unfaithfulness you deal,
But from it all God can restore again and heal.
As you move on,
You must forgive the one to you that they have scorn.
It is a painful thing,
But peace to you it will bring.
Stop holding on to the past,
Those memories let them fade and to God cast.
He is your healing process,
So let Him be God so He can bring and
revive you again so you can be bless.

Not every man or woman has a hidden agenda,
And not every man or woman is out to hurt
you again or to be a pretender.
God is love,
And love covers a multitude of sins from
earth to heaven up above.
Love can mend,
And you can find or receive true love again my friend.
Put away the past and in timing put down your guard,
Because when you accept God as your Savior; He
will guide you and be your staff and rod.
Cast away all bitterness, anger, defensiveness, that
wall that was built, being controlling, your pride,
low self-esteem, and being left and let down,
Because it is not fair to the next man or
woman that God brings around.
In front of you present a diamond in the ruff and gem,
That was once or twice broken and was put out for trash
but is here now to be treasures so don't overlook them.
Everyone is not the same,
There are still some good men and women out there
that are not out to hurt you or play games.
Change must take place,
Because we all can improve and be renewed by
God's mercy and grace.
For a man or a woman to be alone is good for a season,
At some point the two will or shall come together because
that's how God wants it; it's His will and reason.

It's not meant for man to be alone,
But for him to protect, love, provide,
and lead next to God and His Son Jesus that sits on the throne.
Don't ever compare one to another,
Everyone is different just take heed and listen
to the wise word spoken by a mother.
Mothers knows best,
Because they have wisdom and have been thru the test.
Please stay away from negative people and thoughts,
And dwell on the positive things to you that God has brought.
Remember misery likes company you know,
So stop letting people talk in your ear about what you
should or should not do or what direction you should go.
Just follow God and your heart,
Starting over is not a bad thing becoming friends is a start.
So don't give up on love because it and
God hasn't given up on you,
There's still a great person out there that is true.
Just like surgery you can heal, be restructured,
have a replacement, and have something negative
removed by a scalpel and with sutures,
So don't let your past predict your future.

Winning Season

The time has come,
For me to reap and from my pain, hurt, and suffering
my history is where it's coming from.
Now I will receive the harvest,
God is showing and giving me His best.
For all the tears,
Here comes the joy to bring cheers.
God never forgets,
So to be established the going thru He had to let.
I'm holding on,
Because my patience will let me get my reward from my scorn.
It may not have come when I wanted it to,
That's why Lord,
I surrender myself to you.
Trust, wait, and endure,
Jesus will show up for sure.
My trials, storms, humbleness, and faithfulness are my reasons,
To know that I'm in my winning season.

No Time For

Pointing fingers and placing blame,
Or the nonsense or games.
Any drama in my day,
That's why it's so very important to pray.
People with their judgement and criticism,
And those who always want to be the victim.
The negative talk or vibes,
Because greatness to me God has subscribe.
Casting stones,
Then I rather be alone.
The past holding,
Forgive and move on because God is the Potter
and He is always molding.
The distraction,
Be led by God He's your action.
To moping,
Strength, power, favor, joy, mercy, and grace are your coping.
Anyone's mess,
Because God is here to bless.
You to pretend,
Give it to Jesus He heals, delivers, and mends.
The selfish way you live,
To another give.

Keeping it all for you,
Share, pour into, and bless others that's
what God anointed you to do.
The gossip talk,
With Jesus walk.
Looking back,
Use wisdom, knowledge, common sense,
and the word to overcome your lack.
Saying you can't,
You can do all things through Christ that strengthens you,
so have faith even if it's as small as an ant.
Lingering and procrastination,
Equity and work are your dedication.
Into my destiny and blessings,
I want to soar, So negativity and unbelief I have no time for.

Expect The Turn Around

Even when you are down and out,
In God's timing He will give you a reason to shout.
You can be picked up from the ground,
And become again profound.
There is a way,
It starts when you pray.
Things you will go thru,
But trusting in God is what you have to do.
Testing you is what God does,
He wants you to see and know that you can get pass the was.
I know at some point you may want to break,
But remain humble and a blessing God will make.
You could be damage goods,
But God can mold you back as you should.
Anything that was lost or stolen will be found,
So your blessing expect in the turn around.

Trust And Believe

Know that you are a gem,
And any obstacles and challenges you can overcome them.
In yourself know that you can do all things,
And greatness to you the Lord shall bring.
Don't let anything get you down,
And know that God will turn things around.
When you are going thru,
Activating your faith you must do.
God wants you to depend solely on Him,
He is your light to your dim.
Circumstances will be your test and will run its course,
But just remember that God is your source.
Even though right now you are robbing Peter to pay
Paul and money is looking strange,
See past that because your finances will change.
On the rise healing is done,
And the victory is won.
Past the pain and struggles you will see,
Strength, dominion, power, determination,
and self-confidence are mighty in thee.
This is not the time to give up,
God is waiting on you so He can filleth up your cup.
So of yourself and God don't deceive,
In the two trust and believe.

To Please My Audience

My creativity is to reach others,
To save a marriage, to encourage the hopeless, to
inspire the doubtful, to support the lost,
to comfort the broken and see friends and family
come together like daughters and mothers.
Even when the romance is not as nice,
I write something to turn up the heat again with a lot of spice.
On different levels people I meet,
To captivate them with my words make them complete.
Some people need to be reminded,
Because they forget, get caught up, been down,
listened to the wrong voice and been blinded.
My poetry is their rescue,
To shed light and provide a positive view.
We all can use some help every once in a while,
That's where my art comes into play to create smiles.
I always tell people with my poetry don't judge me,
I'm reaching everyone in any way possible that concept see.
Some people need Jesus in their life,
I use my inspiration to help them see thru their strife.
Others need a push from hurt, pain, disappointment,
and brokenness on how to move on,
I've been there so I write to dissolve their scorn.

I comfort some with death they face,
My words bring peace and grace.
My favorite is to tell about and express
love because love I'm truly about,
And when I write to advocate it there will be no doubt.
Some just need a thank you and I appreciate you,
Thoughtfulness I do.
Just ask I will make a way,
For Weddings, Funerals, Holidays, Graduations, Anniversaries,
Just Because and Birthdays.
Even to make out of things sense,
I'm here to please my audience.

Be Positive

Create it as your lifestyle,
And more smile.
We may not always see eye to eye or agree,
But it's about coming together to produce
good results so a solution we can see.
We all go thru things in life,
But we have to see pass the strife.
Don't get caught up in the wrong or dark
but see the better the light,
And work towards what's better for
others and to do what's right.
It's about creating a way,
And from negativity stray.
Something upbeat and good to the table we should bring,
And fairness, understanding, and compromising is the thing.
The atmosphere should always have a good vibe,
So being happy, having great discussions, and
making success happen we subscribe.
It's not about you or me,
It's about making others feel appreciated
and our thoughtfulness is the key.
What's best is what we are seeking to find,
So be optimistic and humble and keep a clear mind.

Step out of you,
And consider and respect everyone's view.
We are all in this together,
So with all the ideas, creativity, and options we
are listening to see what will work better.
We all could have been anywhere,
But we chose to help, volunteer, get involve,
and be a part of a team that's why we are here.
Let us not get so in tuned in our known
personal emotions and feelings,
It's all about solution seeking, having fun while doing it, creating
laughter, making new acquaintances, and bringing healing.
Today this is how we should live,
So let's be positive.

It Takes

A simple hello,
And being kind to the next fellow.
For you to say thank you,
And for another do.
A smile for you to give,
And a step forward each day to better live.
Something kind to say,
And for others pray.
A team,
To come together to produce the dream.
Love coming from you,
And to others being true.
Forgiveness to heal,
So better we can feel.
A hug,
So a comfort and encouragement on others can snug.
You and me,
So results we can see.
Faith to make it,
And trusting and believing God every bit.
Having a pure heart,
Being grateful, humble, giving, and faithful is where it starts.
Positive decisions make,
This is what it takes.

Shavetta Craig

Sunshine And Sunflowers

It's to be bright,
To add color and create light.
It bring happiness to the day,
And peace and a shine your way.
Hope is on the arise,
With goodness to be wise.
The rays and beauty they seek,
As a refreshing and positive vibes peaks.
The color yellow gives it meaning to see,
To explore greatness in your life to be.
Its purpose is to bring joy,
And anything negative it will destroy.
What a great combination,
To bring back life to the nation.
They bring a smile to your face,
And fills you with grace.
It puts you in a good mood,
And energize you with this amazing attitude.
For growth it has to be showers,
And then you are blessed with sunshine and sunflowers.

Smile

For another day,
And to God you get to pray.
The great people in your life that entered,
And the great memories remembered.
For the life that you have,
And always creating laughs.
To the kind words,
And the wonderful things that you accomplished and heard.
To a forever friend,
Who will cherish everything about you and love to the end.
To the children you created,
And to goals, dreams, achievements, faith and hope anticipated.
To the lessons learned,
And greatness and something better to yearn.
For you Jesus went the extra mile,
Just for being thankful, grateful and humble always smile.

Shavetta Craig

To Encourage You

In your life there may be a cloud,
But shout I have the victory loud.
You may be annoyed,
But God will fill the void.
Things may seem complex,
Just know for a blessing you are next.
From the storm,
A new thing in you God will form.
I know you are scorn,
Just hold on.
Yes a mess of your life you have made,
Forgive and repent as the hurt,
pain and brokenness fades.
How you are going to make it you don't know,
Trust God and go with His flow.
It's like you do good then you trip,
The scene for you God will flip.
Your burdens weigh heavy to carry,
It will be lifted from our right on time God though it tarry.
You will endure sunshine and gray,
But you will make it thru each day.
God has you and thru anything He will see you thru,
It's my assignment to encourage you.

A Breath Of Fresh Air

He is that relief,
And of everything chief.
Just fine I inhale and exhale,
Because for me He prevails.
Having a safety net,
You, I'm glad we met.
The resource I can count on,
That sees me thru the hell and scorn.
From my struggles you give me a release,
And you bring me peace.
When the enemy comes to kill, steal and destroy, you bring me joy.
When my stress level is to the max,
You give me the strength to relax.
When I'm broken or down He repairs,
Jesus a breath of fresh air.

Always

Make others happy,
And thank God snappy.
Put on a smile,
And in you let the Holy Spirit pile.
Say something kind,
And keep a positive mind.
Throughout the day pray,
And for others in need make a way.
Lend a hand,
And for what's right stand.
Tell the truth,
And enjoy your youth.
Make progress,
And do better and aim for success.
Want to improve,
And from the past move.
Be thankful, grateful and sho,
And know you can make it again from a humble.
Say thank you and I love you,
And unexpected things do.
Give respect,
And on great things reflect.
For waking you up and providing for you every day
give God praise,
And be joyful always.

Share And Care

Love one another please,
Giving, inspiring, encouraging, supporting,
and comforting produce these.
We all have needs,
Be the one to step up and help I plead.
We all are a village and family to provide,
And be a light of help to guide.
We face situations every day,
Be the help that is on the way.
For others do, for things like this God created you.
When they are hurt and sore,
Into them pour,
When they don't have a smile on their face,
Show them some kindness with a warm embrace.
Plant seeds,
And reach out indeed.
Life is filled with learning lessons,
But others are equipped to help you in the right direction.
Storms, obstacles, challenges, trials and tribulations
you will endure, so stop stressing,
Because all around you are people to be a blessing.
You don't know what a person is battling with or what's
tearing them apart,
So do with you can from your heart.
It doesn't take much,
Whatever you do that person will be touched.
For another be there,
So share and care.

Do I

Have it all together,
No but I strive to do better.
Make all the time the right choices,
No but I try to differentiate the two
between God and the enemy voices.
Always do right,
No I sometimes lose sight but I look to
God to be my guide and light.
Always be happy,
No but I get back to being very snappy.
Always love as I should,
No but I show improvement every day I could.
Make mistakes,
Yes but God still blesses me even though me He breaks.
Sometimes sin,
Yes but I ask for forgiveness and repent and
God creates a new image within.
Fall short,
Yes but I will never give up or on my dream abort.
Have doubts and stumble,
Yes but I remain humble.
Fail Jesus,
Yes but there is a turnaround, change, and shift in all of us.

Deserve what Jesus does for me,
No but I still give Him the glory.
Have the right to judge,
No we are all sinners and are imperfect,
so from the negativity budge.
Worry and doubt,
Yes but having faith and trusting God is what it's about.
Want to give up and cry,
Sometimes but God says you shall live and not die.
Always have a smile on my face,
No but I get one quick so goodness on someone else I can embrace.
Lord for you and others I try,
So do I.

Shavetta Craig

That Moment

For a while the storms, burdens, trials, tribulations,
challenges, and troubles we carry,
Be still and know,
And continue to let our faith grow.
Just don't quit, it surely, we will get.
The reaping on us will sneak,
So don't draw weary or become weak.
We don't see it because it's in a disguise,
God's timing is perfect it always catches us by surprise.
It's going to happen and be a shock,
It's happening for us my word mock.
We are going to say Wow,
As the blessings-on-blessings God allows.
The miracles and the impossible are going
to make us speechless, bless.
It will have us in a trance and paralyze,
As God has done above all we could ask or think we realize.
This time the weeping will be because of joy of the blessings sent,
God is about to show us who He is in that moment.

It's Time To De

It shall and will be done,
And it can only be done by you, God, you are The One.
Detach people and things,
And something rewarding and refreshing bring.
And renew what's pleasant to see.
Deliver us from evil and what's trying to take us out,
Restoration is what it's all about.
Derail what's coming against,
And remind us that your will and way God is what makes sense.
Decisions to be made, and remembering the price paid.
Develop something new,
Deposit into us what will make us great,
Realign us as in you God we trust and wait.
And let us defeat the battles ahead,
And let us reconnect with you God, led.
Delete all that was and is not good,
And regain our faith in God as we should.
As it's time to die.

Shavetta Craig

In With The New

Future shall be,
And blessings you will see.
Rewarding beginnings,
And getting to your winnings.
Life to embark,
And creating love to spark.
Path to take,
And great decisions to make.
A mind,
And purpose to find.
The positive thoughts,
And the miracles and impossible brought.
To what was say goodbye,
And what's in front of you and ahead try.

It Won't Last Always

Troubles will come but they will go,
Better is coming this I know.
Storms will brew,
But you will get through.
Challenges will try to defeat you,
But winning you will do.
And get you to your prospective place,
And blessings to embrace.
Negativity is not for you to dwell in and see,
So stay positive and the miracles will be.
The sour will turn to bring out the best,
You are just going through a test.
What's wrong will turn,
And you will have what you yearn.
Silence in timing it will speak,
And what you ask it will peak,
Confusion, doubt, and overthinking comes to be a pollution,
Clarity and faith are the solution.
Difficulties will not have residence in you,
Because the impossible God will do.
So thank God and give Him praise,
Because the bad that is happening to you it won't last always.

We All Have A Sin

Trying to live and do right each day,
But if we don't know anything else we know how to pray.
We battle with different things,
As we still have a purpose and assignment
that's why we haven't gained our wings.
Perfect we will never be,
But forgiveness and seeking God is our destiny.
We face, fight and wrestle with so much,
But we can be healed, delivered, and set freed by God's touch.
But God is the only way,
Thru the wrong, temptation, ugly and worse the
choice is by Him and with Him to stay.
We are a daily process,
And by God's will, we will be bless.
We get over one and stumble over another,
But keep praying for your sisters and brothers.
We will come out of this and win,
So put God first as we all have a sin.

Strong

Through the acts of pain,
Faithful I still remain.
The different levels of hurt,
Made me feel unworthy and like dirt.
All the tears I cry and constantly weeping,
The promises and joy will come for me to be reaping.
When they can't see,
I'm still there for thee.
I continue to stumble,
But my spirit keeps me humble.
Things try to keep me down,
I still smile to hide my frown.
Numerous times I have been broken,
But I have to wait and trust in God to do what He has spoken.
Sometimes having patience is hard to do,
The unseen kicks in that faith in my view.
But I do all I can my life is in lack and despair,
But I do all I can to show and share with others
that I care and that we both can repair.
When things in my life are blocked,
From my tears and sweat with hope I have to build a solid rock.
When they keep saying no,
I have to believe, declare, receive, and claim that it is so.

When my feelings start to rust,
I need the oil and continue to trust.
When I'm torn inside,
The spirit rises up in me and glides.
When I can't see a way, The only thing to do is pray.
When of me they mock,
All I know to do is ask, seek, and knock.
When I want to throw in the towel and let go of the rope,
Now I have activated my hope.
When on life I say I'm thru,
Then God speaks and says there is more work for you to
do and your test and testimony is for others not you.
The rejection, obstacles, challenges, and storms doesn't seem fair,
But God said 'He wouldn't give it to me if I couldn't bear.
I don't know if I'm coming or going,
But mercy and favor on me is still glowing.
Thou it tarry wait for it, it may prolong,
Thru it all I will and shall remain and stay strong.

Sunny Days

Great things are on the horizon,
And all things are possible to your surprising.
Your problems will go with the setting of the sun,
And for you victory was won.
The wait is over for you,
God is going to show you what He can do.
For your patience you will be rewarded,
God is pleased I will bless you as He told it.
The storms are about to blow away, and God is
answering your prayers that you prayed.
Things again will be bright,
No more darkness so see the light.
Your faith stood strong,
Even when things went wrong.
God is showing up in many ways,
To bring back again sunny days.

I Love To Create Smiles

We all have our good and bad days,
But in some type of way I love to give others praise.
When frustration builds up you frown,
My talents I use to turn things around.
Happiness in others I love to see,
It's like honey producing from a bee.
When something in your heart tugs,
I'm ready to encourage you with a hug.
Every day won't be grand,
But right by you I will stand.
When you need to vent,
I'm right here heaven sent.
When you fear,
I will have something to say to bring cheer.
I was blessed with a gift,
Others spirits to uplift.
Making others shine is my charm, and loving
them and embracing them in my arms.
I don't want to see anything make you disappointed or mad,
Because I'm going to do everything I can to make you again glad.
When in me you confide,
I will brighten you and what you told in my heart I hide.
All my goodness on others I will pile,
As I love to create smiles.

Beauty

Is your value,
And a true virtue.
It is created for good,
And bask in it as you should.
It's a special art,
And it develops from the heart.
And it glows on your life and chin,
It's the image to you and creates a spin.
That gives to you that was given,
That gives you a purpose for living.
It's an amazing thing,
And something miraculous to you it brings.
Your spirit should always be on duty,
Because it's what creates your beauty.

Shavetta Craig

Undecided

Patience is a virtue,
While waiting great things will come to you.
Which way to go,
Let your heart show you so.
Who truly cares,
You are fully aware.
You have to follow faith the unseen,
And towards happiness and love lean.
Wrong or right,
No one's perfect on what matters don't lose sight.
What does your heart yearn,
That's the direction to turn.
By God be guided,
What you should do He already provided.
In my life you are invited,
While you are undecided.

A Ray

Is who I am,
And gentle and peaceful like a lamb.
A reason to smile,
As greatness on you I pile.
Making countless efforts that things will be fine,
That's why I'm called Sunshine.
In lives I spark,
I'm light to the dark.
A sensational additive,
And always smiling and positive.
To make you shine like the sun,
It's me I'm the one.
Created to brighten the day,
That's me a ray.

We

Aren't bad we just make bad choices,
We have a problem discerning between the evil and wise voices.
All do wrong,
But who will repent and ask for forgiveness and
work towards doing right and staying strong?
All know what to do,
We have to activate our faith and work
on ourselves and to God be true.
Have to stop judging one another,
And love, support and encourage your friend, sister, or brother.
Have lacks,
But we have to be motivated to get our lives on track.
Have to stick together,
It's what God wants and it's the only
way to make this world better.
All have failed a time or two,
We must learn from the mistakes and not repeat
the same, yes this is for me and you.
Always got an excuse,
So content, sticking with what we know, afraid of change,
not thinking outside of the box; instead of letting our
self-esteem, determination and willpower run loose.
Don't have to match,
But to each other we need to latch.
Need to help, care, and be there for another when we can,
And be the greatest person, leader or role
model and follow God's plan.
Need to stop being selfish thinking it's all about I or me,
It takes a team, village, family, and community.
Someone different and unusual we need to become and see,
It's not you or me, it's we.

One Day

The rain of storms will stop,
And blessings will constantly drop.
Comfort will find you,
And great things you will achieve and do.
Happiness will rise,
Life greatness will catch you off guard and by surprise.
And love will discover you and stay grounded forever,
and your dreams will become your future endeavors.
You will think and look back,
And say thank you Jesus, I made it no more lacks.
Your tears will be for good reasons,
Be patient you are about to walk into your season.
Your heart will shine, and everything will fall in line.
They will come back to you,
and starting over to make togetherness new.
You will see the light,
And give up on the darkness to do right.
It just takes you to pray,
And you will see things happen one day.

Attention

Fix what's broke,
And listen to your heart that spoke.
Focus on what matters, and repair what shatters.
Love more needs to be shown, and our maturity grown.
Hobbies, careers, and entertainment you love to do,
But right there at home your priceless moments
with family should be your view.
You are always on the go,
It's time to take things slow.
Choose the right road,
And release that heavy load.
To your home God has you confined,
So you can understand and see what's more important
and transform your thinking and mind.
Correct the harm,
This pandemic is the alarm.
The good revisit,
And remember who is still there for you and on them don't quit.
No more extensions,
Let's get it right this time because God is
tired of trying to get our attention.

I'm Therapy

Do you want to sit and talk,
Or release your thoughts with a walk.
It's between you and me your confessions,
And you will have my undivided attention thru the sessions.
I will listen to you,
To advise you of wisdom to do.
My words to you I want them to reach,
To mend and heal and not to judge or preach.
I want to get to the root,
And the negativity boot.
Letting you see your situation in a different light,
And it's not about saying that you are wrong or right.
For people I care for and love so much,
And by my inspiration and encouragement
I want them to be touch.
I want to discover the best and greatness of you,
Want I see and bring out I want you to receive it to.
My hugs bring a needed release,
That helps you live in peace.
Sometimes nothing you don't have to say,
Because I already know and for you, I pray.
An answer you are not always looking for,
The fact that I can smile at you is a solution for you to adore.
I am blessed with a personality and a charm,
That eases a person when challenges and situations cause a harm.
I'm no miracle worker or celebrity,
I'm an average woman and I'm therapy.

There Is A Way

When a car is broke,
You do the repairs to make it awoke.
When you have an injury,
You can get better with surgery.
From a heartbreak,
You can resuscitate.
From a mistake,
Better decisions you can make.
You can fail,
And again prevail.
So when a relationship or marriage goes sour,
You can give it back again power.
When you fall,
Get back up again and give it your all.
When something is dry,
Water to it you can apply.
To heal, try and stay,
There is a way.

To Build You

I want you to become someone greater,
Encourage you to see your dreams and
goals to create now than later.
To do whatever it takes,
And your bright future we can make.
To you I want to add,
Where I'm strong use it to strengthen you to make you glad.
Our actions we need to show to get things back in line and right,
And on what truly matters let that be our sight.
I want to see you succeed,
And assist you with your needs.
When we focus on building and pushing each other to do more
to form a solid foundation and structure it will fit like a glove,
Then everything else will fall into place especially love.
And doing for you without the ask,
That lets you know that I'm willing to help you excel in any task.
To be the match that lights you,
And let you know that anything you can do.
Letting my heart and motivation be your guide,
And my thoughtfulness, faithfulness,
and willingness I will provide.
My inspiration, support, willpower, passion,
dedication, and positive vibes are what I do,
To build you.

It's To

Change the wrong not the good,
And do what you should and could.
Prosper and gain,
And the same not remain.
See things differently,
And wanting to do a makeover, revision
And transform are the key.
Give and do,
And share a gift from you.
Lead the blind,
And let your heart be easy to find.
Show your best,
And put your goodness to the test.
Be thankful every day,
And for one another pray.
Make wise choices,
And adhere to positive voices.
Display your worth and virtue,
Because your action it's to.

You Can

Start over again,
Fix, rebuild, repair, restore and mend.
Pick up the pieces and put them back together,
And learn from the mistakes and make things this time better.
Make things right,
And not dwell again in the things that made you lose sight.
Love the same,
But this time without the hurt, shame and games.
Fight for love,
Because he or she you are still thinking of.
Do and accomplish what you put your mind to,
Effort, trying, and actions starts with you.
Forgive and move on,
And stop dwelling on the mistakes and the scorn.
Remold what you broke,
Because someone else emotions and feelings are not a joke.
In a problem be the solution,
Regardless of who caused the pollution.
Be honest with yourself and others and speak your mind,
And hope, peace, love, happiness, laughter,
and togetherness regain and find.
Transform your way of thinking and mindset,
And release yourself of your past and forget.

Do it,
So in your dreams, growth, opportunities and
with that one you love don't quit.
For yourself change,
Even if it feels or seems strange.
Be great,
Your goodness create.
Overcome trials and storms,
So your faith form.
Take that step and do this,
And go after what you miss.
Speak up and share,
and show that you truly care.
Stand up and rise,
Because you are important, special, gifted and
bring meaning and that's no surprise.
Correct, solve, bend, and errors pan,
There's no such thing as can't, know you can.

Family

We will have our ups and downs,
And will have laughter and frowns.
Love is crucial, important, vital, needed and is the token,
It has the power to fix what's broken.
Love never fades,
A permanent fixture and dwelling place
in each other's lives it made.
It's not about being single,
With endurance, a lifetime, committing and not giving up mingle.
It's where your heart is,
They need you to be that father or mother and hers or his.
Even with some alone time or a break,
Steps forward to mending, making up, forgiving,
changing, and improving are the measures to take.
It should be your main concern, and from the past
mistakes learn and those you left yearn.
Is a longevity bond,
Worth fighting for and to it stay fond.
you need them and they need you,
Taking the time to make it right do.
Together we are supposed to be,
So reconnect and reconcile with your family.

Shavetta Craig

No Perfect Human Being

We don't think before we speak,
And we have habits and temptations that makes us weak.
We fall short and sin,
And wrong directions and places we have been.
We have a flaw or two,
And we have a bad habit to judge and talk about what others do.
We tell lies, cheat, and steal, and we fear, worry,
stress, get depressed and have a hard time to heal.
We start things but don't finish,
And our attention span is short and if it doesn't happen
right away, we just let the thought or dream diminish.
We try and fail, and give up too easily without
the willpower to do it again to prevail.
We let low self-esteem, self-pity and no
confidence define and take control of us,
And we feel that the solution to the problem is to
get revenge, blame, argue, cuss and fuss.
We doubt than to believe,
And we don't want to give; we just want to receive.
We are ready to fight,
And talk more about someone's wrong than what they do right.
All we care about is I, me, or money,
And we don't take things serious enough, we think it's funny.
We have to rise from these ways of being and thinkings,
Or we will continue in these negative ways be sinking.
Correction, change, a turnaround, doing better, mentality shift,
improvement, achieving, striving and a 360 are for seeing,
Because there is no perfect human being.

Life's Too Short

To give up on a dream,
And stop being a team.
To hold on to hurt and mistakes,
And not willing to mend a heartbreak.
For you not to try,
And do all you can before you die.
To just sit around,
Enjoy life and living create something profound.
To be bitter,
Forgive and be forgiven and go get him or her.
To hold grudges and be mad,
You were blessed with another day so be glad.
To stress, worry or mope,
Be thankful, humble, grateful, and live with faith and hope.
Tomorrow is not promised to me or you,
Captivate the moments and something great do.
On love don't abort,
Because life's too short.

Shavetta Craig

Don't Dwell

In misery,
Something brighter and better see.
In the hurt and pain, you been thru,
Healing you do.
In darkness,
So let your light shine because you were built for success.
In what people do or say,
Do you and positive stay.
In the mud,
Grow and rise from your bud.
In sorrow,
Soar for a better tomorrow.
In yesterday,
It's gone so let your future lead the way.
On what was done wrong,
Learn from it and correct it and continue to stay strong.
From your storms you will have a story to tell,
So in your past don't dwell.

It's Worth Fighting For

Life is like a jigsaw puzzle in timing you figure
it out and put the pieces together in place,
And difficulties and challenges you face.
Some things don't deserve the pause,
Regardless of the cause.
For the breath given,
Have a purpose for living.
Just know love is not to fail,
It's equipped to sail.
What was developed let it sustain,
Weather it out and let love remain.
Love is concrete,
As it is profound and solid to make every and anything complete.
Love doesn't expire,
So keep it lite like a fire.
Don't just dream make it a reality,
Because to achieve you have the ability.
Don't let it just be a thought,
Let your actions be brought.
Don't let your past and mistakes define you,
Because anything or anyone can become new.
Never give up so do, give and expect more,
Life, love, and the future it's worth fighting for.

Shavetta Craig

It Will Happen For You

Your dream to have,
And to love to bear and to always laugh.
That major change,
And the impossible even if it seems strange.
The unfolding of something great,
As a new thing God creates.
Better to come from your past,
With blessings to last.
The prayers you said,
And healing from the many scars you bled.
When you surrender,
It will flee the things that holds you back, keeps you
confined, takes control of you and the hinder.
A reset and fresh start,
And serving your purpose and doing your part.
To rid the strife,
That attacks your life.
The increase, overflow, winning season, and breakthrough,
Just wait as it will happen for you.

Life's Struggles

Are a wakeup call,
And giving you common sense from your falls.
Gives a reaction for you to bounce back,
And not to retrace your tracks.
Seems to happen more than few,
But getting back up, starting over, and
getting another chance is on you.
It's a lesson learned,
As changes you yearn.
They can cut and burn,
But it gives you the opportunity in your
life to make the needed turn.
Will whip you every time,
But those scars and bruises created growth
to get you to your prime.
It can be a beast,
It keeps coming for you but you aren't
trying to lose to say the least.
It wants you to accomplish and finish the race,
So overcome the challenges and obstacles you face.
Hard they can be,
But a better and brighter future you can see.

Don't back down, the situation defeat,
So you can stay grounded on your feet.
A solution you search and money you scrape,
As the problems you try to escape.
Makes success seems so far away,
But to making it some day you can't stray.
It blows up in your face like dust,
So brush yourself off and continue forward, believe and trust.
It came to destroy,
But it will fail because it's for you to have happiness and joy.
It comes to kill so you won't survive,
But you are built to thrive.
It really attacks deep,
But a healing and reward you will reap.
It will create an anthem,
From crumbles it will produce gems.
You become a pro on how to juggle,
The different life's struggles.

Don't Take Anything For Granted

The shoes on your feet,
And your heartbeats.
The love shown,
And the thoughtfulness known.
The food on the table,
To walk, talk, see, and hear you are able.
That thank you,
And I appreciate what you do.
A smile that you share, and showing someone that you care.
The life that you have,
And the ability to laugh.
A place to sleep,
And favor that makes you reap.
The purpose to thrive, and the car that you drive.
To blink,
And a thought to think.
The child that you birth,
And your time on earth.
The money that you do make,
And be humble for the chicken when you can't have steak.
The one that has your back,
Even when you lack.
Ungratefulness could have it fade or taken away,
So count your blessings every day.
All the good that is planted,
So don't take anything for granted.

Shavetta Craig

Do More

The answer is to give,
And thru your actions live.
Bring a smile to a face,
Your all from procrastination replace.
Effort show, It's the way to grow.
Time spend, Brokenness mend.
Your hand reach out,
And let the greatest in you spout.
Speak what you feel,
And use your gift to heal.
Hug and kiss,
And display that them who you miss.
Trying and doing provide,
And what's truly inside don't hide.
Come around a lot,
And really give it everything you got.
Do don't just say,
And express something every day.
Encouragement and comfort others need,
You don't know the hurt and pain they go
thru and how their inside bleeds.
Give that push and support,
Someone just want to know and feel that you are in their court.
Give and you will receive,
And listen, trust, and believe.
Your love and feelings pour,
And of yourself do more.

You Are Too Close

The enemy can't have you,
Because there is still work for you to do.
Heavy may be your burdens and weight,
But you are approaching something great.
You must finish strong,
So forget about your past, sins, and the
things you have done wrong.
It's time to come face to face with your yet,
To see the wonderful things and blessings you haven't met.
You can't give up now,
Get back up from your down.
Crawl, push, pull, grab, and hold on don't stop,
You are getting there your faith don't drop.
Don't quit on what you dreamed for,
Motivation, trust, belief,
and willpower will give you the progress to soar.
The light see,
Don't let darkness, fear and doubt defeat thee.
It may seem like a long time coming,
To the promise keep running.

You may be faced with the fog, glare, and the dim,
Just know you can go straight through them.
You keep saying why are these troubles, storms and
tribulations always happening to me,
Because ahead greater awaits for you to see.
What you face will hurt, bring pain, downpour of tears and
make you want to quit but it you carry,
You are there the rewards for your faithfulness
and continuing will not tarry.
Continue to trust God and give Him your most,
Because to your harvest and your season you are too close.

It Was Given

Life for you to have,
And the ability to laugh.
Love for you to sustain and enjoy,
To build and become stronger and not to destroy.
Peace to clear your mind,
With joy to find.
Happiness to embrace,
And much mercy and grace.
The favor on you,
And greatness to do.
Light to lead you in the right direction,
And angel to be your protection.
The power to speak,
And improvement seek.
To look and see,
The great things God has done for thee.
Another breathing day,
And the confidence to pray.
Find purpose and meaning while you are living,
These things were added unto you it was given.

Shavetta Craig

Put It Away

Bad thoughts,
And the hurt it brought.
Childish ways and things,
Be and act mature and change bring.
The sour feelings,
And become kind and find healing.
All the temptations and hinderance,
And do better with perseverance.
All negativity that has you bound,
And let positivity and determination be found.
The laziness, contentment, procrastination, and doubt,
Smile and be happy no more pout.
The jealousy and envy,
And the temptations that afflicts thee.
The silence,
And any verbal or physical violence.
Being unstable and confused,
The right choices choose.
Older you are getting so let an effect of
transformation in you start today,
As the former you put it away.

Thank You For The Re

A new story I will rewrite,
Erasing the past and doing things right.
A chance to review where I went wrong,
To teach me how to stay strong.
Letting the good about me remain,
And revealing the best in me so it can sustain.
From my brokenness I resuscitate,
With a new image to create.
Life takes a revision,
And cancel separation and division.
Reunite love and hearts,
Forgiving and moving forward together is the start.
Reconnect what was lost,
And do it at all cost.
Restructure what failed,
Build back again because things can prevail.
Restrain from the things that caused the harm,
And embrace change with open arms.
What's losing life revive,
Rejuvenate and bring it back alive.
Anything you can redo,
It starts with you.
Great again you can be,
Lord thank you for the re.

It's Never Too Late

To be in love again,
Starting fresh as you mend.
To start a new career,
And work on your fears.
To go back to school,
No matter your age you will always be cool.
Bad habits put away,
And make a difference every day.
To fix what's broken,
Forgiving and creating something new is the token.
To win,
Never give up even when your faith is thin.
For your dream to be,
When you put your mind to it anything you can see.
To walk down that aisle,
And have a reason again to smile.
To rewrite your story,
And this time without a worry.
When on God you wait,
The greatest blessing will happen to you
something you never anticipate.
For emotions to feel,
And from a bad situation heal.

To say I love you, and I apologize for the hurt and pain I did too.
To put pieces back together, and make life better.
To say goodbye,
To things that continue to make you cry.
To let someone have your heart,
Being friends and trusting again is how it starts.
Just know that change is great,
Regardless of the length of time it's never too late.

It's Your Job

When you see the warning signs you go to a mechanic,
When they check and repair it comes automatic.
For a first responder or fireman to rescue,
Their objective is to save you.
To appraise to know the value to expect,
To ensure that it's next to perfect.
Lessons to teach,
With words to reach.
A lifeguard to help you not to drown,
Stay afloat in life you can turn things around.
Get a doctor to perform surgery,
And some physical therapy to aide thee.
To be a player on the team,
And encouraging someone else to fulfill their dreams.
Everyone has a duty to do,
Because someone is counting on you.
To change, fix, replace, and restore turn the knob,
To do something different and make a difference it's your job.

Kill Them With Kindness

When others are mean,
On love you lean.
No matter of others attitude,
You remain in a good mood.
When they are not nice or kind,
Goodness in your heart you still find.
Two wrongs don't make a right,
You give happiness, joy, forgive and shed light.
When they are bitter,
Show how to be at peace, care and not be a quitter.
Even if they envy you,
Smiling you continue to do.
When upon you they frown,
Show them that friendliness, care, concern,
and positivity is how you get down.
Even with afflictions, habits, flaws, and mess,
Always kill them with kindness.

Stay In Your Lane

If it doesn't concern you,
Stay out of it because there is nothing for you to do.
Others business and what they do stay out,
What you do just be about.
Your focus shouldn't be about what others are doing,
What you are here to do please keep pursuing.
And stop looking for trouble and causing blame,
We are all adults so stop playing the snitching,
kissing up and tata telling game.
What's done in the dark will come to light,
So minding your own business is what's doing right.
We focus on the wrong things,
Peace, comfort, and love to each other we should bring.
Silent learn to be that way,
And know when to talk and when to have nothing to say.
Bring to the equation joy,
Because with your negativity, nosey spirits,
diarrhea of the mouth others mood, happiness,
and attitude you destroy.
If you are keeping your eyes on others then you are not doing
what you are supposed to be doing during the day,
If you are that concern and want to help for them pray.
Your gossip, trying to be in control, pointing fingers and your
he say she say can cause damage and a lot pain,
So do yourself and everyone else a favor and stay in your lane.

No Matter

How hard things gets,
Love the one you're with.
See things thru,
Because someone truly loves you.
When they will help produce your dream,
That's the type of person you want on your team.
They always stayed,
And for you they constantly prayed.
When they are there,
So what will it take for you to do right and be fair.
How many times you fall,
Just don't stay down get back up and give it your all.
Why things happen and fail,
There is a reason for things but just don't give up hope
and faith even when it's moving like a snail.
Fix what's broken and shatters,
Do whatever it takes no matter.

Shavetta Craig

In Your Back Pocket

Don't worry or fear,
Because in some type of way I'm near.
Feel my residue,
As it is with you.
Let my inspiration and encouragement linger,
I'm connected to you like a hand to fingers.
My spirit always carry around,
As the thoughts of me will help you when you are feeling down.
Just know you got this,
As my comfort and support are like a mist.
I'm the rainbow to the rain,
And the needed touch to your pain.
I will be the calm to your storm,
As smiles to your face, I will form.
My voice will bring you ease,
So relax please.
I'm your energy to a socket,
So think of me in your back pocket.

Because Of Your Scars

Don't become bitter,
Continue to move on and be a go getter.
Don't develop anger and rage,
Learn from them and start a new chapter and turn the page.
Don't hold a grudge,
It will take time to heal so from the hurt budge.
Don't remain sour,
Breathe again and let the pain devour.
In them don't dwell,
And you will become strong again with a story to tell.
Don't hold on,
Let go of the scorn.
For a reason or sometimes intentional they were made,
With any set back with timing it will fade.
Focus on the good and not your bad,
And dwell on what makes you happy and not sad.
As you age each year,
With growth and maturity put away the
memories, doubts, and fears.
Don't put your tragedies, mistakes, and bleeds on replay,
From the damage done forgive and stray away.
Don't suffer,
Let them help you to become better and tougher.
Continue to fulfill your dreams and shot for the stars,
Don't let anything stop you because of your scars.

I See You

Every day you rise,
To accomplish a purpose and you do it
with honor which is no surprise.
Everyone you greet,
And there's not a stranger you wouldn't meet.
You keep a smile on your face,
And you stay in a happy place.
You always give one hundred percent,
Doing what you do, creating a laugh,
being helpful and giving your all are how
Your day and time is spent.
You have such a great heart inside,
Kindness and care you share and don't hide.
You are like light,
You make the day bright.
You go the extra mile,
In the rain, cloudy, snow, hot and cold and you still smile.
Others may see it as a paycheck but you see it as a pleasure,
Because you trust in God who blesses you each day with treasures.
You are an inspiration to see,
As it brings joy and happiness to me.
Thank you for showing up each day,
As a great attitude you display.
Gratitude and appreciation for the hard work,
dedication and sacrifice daily that you do,
You won't go unknown because I see you.

We Shall

Score and win,
And rise from where we have been.
Pave the way,
And know how to pray.
Defeat the obstacles that we face,
And change embrace.
Love as God do,
And let kindness be our view.
Stand tall and bold,
And from us greatness will unfold.
Unify as one,
And when we come together the job will get done.
Make some moves,
And what we set our mind to prove.
Show that we can do it,
And we will not quit.
Faith, trust, motivation and are our pal,
Because making a difference,
standing out and being a role model,
we shall.

Shavetta Craig

Why Is It So Hard

Your own business to mind,
And instead of being jealous, a back stabber and
tattletale just learn to be silent and also kind
To be an Indian instead of wanting to be chief,
And to be fair, treat others right and bring to the table relief.
To be one team, and support one another when they
are having a bad day and just need to scream.
For me to defend,
And being true without the pretend.
To come and talk to me,
When a problem you see.
For you to be a solution,
Than causing pollution.
For you to focus and worry about you and stay in your lane,
Instead of causing chaos when it's already a
lot to deal with to try to stay sane.
When you have an issue with me, to me come talk to and ask,
And worry about you and do your task.
Not to be fake and waiver,
Because being two faced is not doing me any favors.

Not to bring extra stress, and to help more and gossip less.
For you to do your job every day,
Instead of stalking like your prey.
To get along,
And do your part and go home and want to fix what's wrong.
To have in the workplace peace,
And all the nonsense cease.
For communication to be a top priority and guard,
And to create change and a positive
environment why is it so hard.

Shavetta Craig

What You Going To Do

Just sit and cry,
Or again try.
Dwell in self-pity,
Or prove yourself to this city.
What you have done so far drop,
Or pick back up achievement and don't stop.
From your problems run,
Or finish and get the job done.
Continue to beg,
Or make it happen with your own two legs.
Are you going to continue to speak hot air,
Or use your actions to make it out there.
Just blow off steam,
Or see it come to pass your dream.
Continue to fall,
Or stand tall.
On your success sleep,
Or elevate and reap.
Keep dwelling on your past,
Or this time make your life a blast.
Are you going to stay down,
Or turn your life around.
The choice is up to you,
So what you going to do?

An Antidote

Hurt, disappointments, pain and burdens you will endure,
But there are solutions to get you thru them for sure.
With a prick from a thorn,
Some care is just needed for the scorn.
For the tears that you cry,
Joy is coming to supply.
For the broken,
Encouragement and mending are the token.
From the scars within,
Inspiration and timing are the best medicine.
When discouragement appears,
Confidence is near.
When you can't cope,
There is hope.
Love is a healing like music notes,
The cure is being an antidote.

Regardless

If you fail, mess up and make mistakes they will still be there,
And always show that they care.
Of what others thinks,
They see the best and better in you and will
pray for you that in your afflictions,
bad habits and addictions you won't sink.
Of how long it takes,
Faith in you they have that the cycle will break.
Of the past that you keep holding on to,
They know one day you will release it and come thru.
Of your dark place,
light you can embrace.
Of what you can't see,
Confidence, a conquer,
to win and to be an achiever are within thee.
Good can come from a bad, demons can flee,
Habits can be changed and failures can create success,
And there is one who will stay to see it happen regardless.

What If

You didn't have any support,
Or someone in your court.
Your cry no one else heard,
And you were speechless without words.
You had to do it alone,
They may be there now but at any time they could be gone.
There wasn't a God to believe in,
And you had to be stuck in sin.
Love was never known,
Or care and kindness to be shown.
You didn't have a choice,
And had to rely on the wrong voice.
The answer was always no, and no direction to go.
All the time you bleed,
And there was no such thing as meeting needs.
Your spirit no one could lift,
And you didn't have a gift.
There wasn't a thing called happiness,
And you never were blessed.
You couldn't think,
And all you did was sink.

Life wasn't given, and you didn't know about living.
You couldn't learn,
And nothing to earn.
You didn't have feelings,
Or options for healing.
Laughter wasn't a thing,
And tears you always bring.
You didn't have the ability to have dreams or believe,
And the capability to receive.
You couldn't move and you were always stiff,
We should be humble, thankful, and grateful because what if.

Be Like A Tree

It is grounded and rooted,
It's like faith it's speaks but it's muted.
It grows and never will be stopped,
It produces again even when chopped.
It has so many resources to provide,
With so much history to guide.
Their leaves come and go,
But their purpose they know.
It's not going anywhere,
No matter what it will always be there.
It's foundation is strong,
And forever last long.
It lives,
And it gives.
It sustains thru all,
Regardless it will remain and stand tall.
It ages,
But still strive and continue on thru its stages.
It's here to help and not hurt,
Even though it's grounded in dirt.
It's a wonderful sight to see,
so be like a tree.

Memories

Something great to have,
To look back on to smile and laugh.
Rewards to hold on to,
That made you.
It's your life in fragments,
And the wonderful ways it complements.
Create so much more,
As it's an amazing thing to adore.
It's like pieces of a dream,
You cherish it and gleam.
It keeps you together,
And makes tomorrow even better.
It's the best thing to reflect,
Enjoy it while you can what the heck.
It's what keeps you going,
And continues happiness flowing.
It keeps us lifted,
And with it we are gifted.
It's our jubilee,
Keep close the memories.

Remember This

Never, can't, and won't, shouldn't be in your vocabulary,
Always persevere, take risks, and be continuous as necessary.
In the impossible believe,
Because things happen surprisingly, unexpectedly,
suddenly, and shockingly so to it cleave.
Always try and don't stop,
And your fears and doubts drop.
God shows you a sign,
So to what is presented to you please don't become blind.
What's truly and genuinely meant for you don't block,
And hold on to and grasp when opportunities knock.
Changes can happen at any time for you,
So embrace the new.
Time will tell,
So let go and let God and in His will dwell.
Good things come to those who wait,
And you can always start over and have a clean slate.
God makes you uncomfortable in the situations,
storms, relationships, and problems current,
Because He wants you to see the best and better that He has sent.
If you are always thinking about them
and they stay on your mind,
Then trust God, your conscience, in what
you feel, and that person find.
To the person that is constantly being there for you,
not giving up on you, believing in you, giving their
all, and to what has started don't dismiss,
Absorb, ponder, think, consider, and accept, so remember this.

Behind The Smile

Are many cries,
Trying not to give up or quit after all the many tries.
The pain that is not shown,
As what's truly going on in their life is not known.
A needed relief,
And overcoming stress, doubt, disappointment, fear, and unbelief.
They cover up the broken heart,
And waiting patiently for the good start.
Anticipating a better day,
Because they don't see a way.
Wondering when the storm and heaviness will cease,
As they need love and peace.
The weariness that causes sleepless nights,
Praying for things to become right.
Things they battle with that you don't see,
So be praying and understanding to thee.
Getting over the past,
And doing your best to have faith and
trust that troubles won't last.
Maintaining with life challenges that pile,
Because of what others don't see behind the smile.

People Need To Hear

I love you,
And God is going to see you through.
Special you are,
And you will go far.
You will get through this,
And your blessings you won't miss.
God has a plan,
So don't believe in your current situation or man.
It's not for you to worry,
Give God the glory because He is writing your story.
You will be blessed,
And God will get you out of this mess.
You are beautiful inside and out,
So don't stress or doubt.
Troubles and storms don't last always,
So, thank God now in advance and give Him praise.
No need to fear,
Are things people need to hear.

Shavetta Craig

Go Through

The hard times to get to the easy,
Your works will pay off eventually you will see.
Bad to get to the good,
And all the pieces will fall together as they should.
Learn from a wrong to get it right,
And what God has for you don't lose sight.
Experience hurt and pain,
But the best and better in your life will sustain.
Enduring scares that leave a mark,
But greatness in your life will spark.
So, what's for you can prepare you to appreciate,
It shows you that timing is everything so wait.
The ugly to see the beauty,
So, faith and perseverance must stay on duty.
By God's glory you will be made perfect,
established, strengthen, and settle you,
After you suffer, wait, and tarry a while
but first you must go through.

Sometimes You Just Have To

Take a risk to see,
What can happen for thee.
Take a chance,
So, with potentials, opportunities, and options dance.
Just do it,
But please don't quit.
Take that leap,
You don't know what you can reap.
See where it will take you,
That attempt do.
Believe and fly,
Every and anything deserves a try.
Take that walk,
And put actions to your talk.
Get up and run,
Live, love, laugh, and have fun.
Trust the process,
Because it's for you to be bless.
Wait your turn,
So, the best and better you can yearn.
Grab their hand and say let's go,
And to forever let's follow.
See it happening for you,
Because sometimes you just have to.

Shavetta Craig

A Negative To A Positive

A bad to a good,
And life will turn out just fine as it should.
From a wrong to a right,
And from darkness you will see light.
A remove to replace,
You are blessed with favor and grace.
A decrease to increase,
Because it's for you to have peace.
We have to resolve to see results,
And aim for better and not focus on the faults.
Something has to detach for something to be deliver,
So, the blessings can reign down on you and flow like a river.
A delay will decree,
So, learn to be still and wait because
something better you will see.
As a denial will declare,
So, your miracles welcome and prepare.
A not so terrific can become great,
Sometimes it has to go through the process so we have to wait.
We have to get up and live,
And turn a negative to a positive.

Time

It doesn't stop, it will always continue and travel,
Along the way things can change and unravel.
It waits for no one,
So live life and have fun.
Always give your best,
And your guard put down, your fears and doubts put to rest.
It continues to accelerate,
So just do it, say yes, try, take risks, seek that chance,
invest, make an attempt, make an exception, and let
it happen it just might make life for you great.
For a reason things happen to and for you,
It's not by accident,
so let it play out and take its course to reveal its purpose
and plan what in your life it's supposed to do.
It doesn't stop or has no brakes,
So let it go and flow even if you make mistakes.
Life will throw curve balls,
So, listen and take heed when options,
opportunities, and potentials falls.
Life is always fill of surprises,
Remember blessings come in disguises.

Don't knock it until you try it,
You just might enjoy it every bit.
You just may discover something new along the way,
As challenges to overcome can happen any day.
It will show,
So, with it grow and know.
It's like not having an expiration date,
So, what's supposed to happen to you let it blossom and generate.
Believe in it and trust it as it will tell,
As it sheds light, makes things clear,
opens your eyes and heart, provides answers,
brings clarity, and brings to your attention what
can make your life better and swell.
Believe in what you write and say,
Because it will produce and progress so with it stay even
while it marinates, slow cook, and bake it won't delay.
At the right moment it will chime,
As it will happen in time.

For The In

In each other we will increase,
And bring multiple things to the table along with peace.
As time goes and we wait something rare and
significant we will initiate,
And it will be solid, so profound, and great.
We will continue to incline,
And we will be just fine.
Interested into each other we will be,
As friendship and relationship, we will see.
I was introduced to you to inspire,
And to be the cause of your fire.
In each other we will take the time to invest,
And become each other's best.
To let each other come inside,
And something everlasting we will provide.
To create love indeed,
And met each other's needs.
Into each other's lives invite,
As what we feel is so right.
To be included in each other's plan,
As I will be your woman and you will be my man.
To inform you we are in this for the win,
As we are for the in.

When We Fail And Fall

To fail is to try again,
And dust yourself off, stand, and mend.
When we fall it's for us to rise,
But this time become wise.
Trials, tribulations, storms, troubles, challenges, obstacles,
and circumstances are the seven we will go through,
We won't stay there it's the lessons to prepare for
the rewards and blessings for us to view.
We have to know about the down to appreciate the getting up,
That's when miracles fill our cup.
Failing and falling are not permanent,
Relief and help will be sent.
Seven times it happened to man,
Now walk into God's plan.
Seven means completion,
Now the wrong and what's trying to come for us is in deletion.
We will get back up and God will give us back all,
When we fail and fall.

Continue To

Smile like you do,
And display the great character of you.
Be gentle and kind,
And peace and happiness find.
Work towards your goals,
And know you have the capability to change souls.
Have fun,
And enjoy life and the sun.
Be positive and true,
And change grey to blue.
Be understanding and willing to learn,
And a blessing in disguise yearn.
Absorb wisdom and be wise,
And be spontaneous and bring a surprise.
Take your time,
And at the right moment things will happen and chime.
Live with purpose and reason,
And be thankful for each day,
minute and second of the seasons.
Be that sunshine ray,
And be who you are every day.
Always do your best and give your all,
And be a support when someone falls.
Be courageous and have wit,
And on nothing quit.
Have patience and wait,
And things will fall into place and will
happen just right and will be great.
To let love be a venue,
Trusting, believing, living, and soaring continue to.

Shavetta Craig

It Was Given

Life for you to have,
And the ability to laugh.
Love for you to sustain and enjoy,
To build and become stronger and not to destroy.
Peace to clear your mind,
With joy to find.
Happiness to embrace,
And much mercy and grace.
The favor on you,
And greatness to do.
Light to lead you in the right direction,
And angels to be your protection.
The power to speak,
And improvement seek.
To look and see,
The great things God has done for thee.
Another breathing day,
And the confidence to pray.
Find purpose and meaning while you are living,
These things were added unto you it was given.

It's About

The purpose to live,
And love to give.
Perseverance each day,
And for others pray.
Maintaining a balance,
And taking a chance.
Making a difference,
And sorting your challenges to make sense.
Being an example,
And supplying kindness ample.
Creating smiles,
And going above and beyond and going the extra mile.
Laughter to make,
And learning from your mistakes.
Giving your all,
And being available to help when someone calls.
The timing, and continue climbing.
Positive vibes,
Hugs, kisses, appreciation,
kind words and care subscribe.
The ability to share, and for whatever comes prepare.
Continuing without the stop,
And know that you will make it to the top.
In yourself believe, and what you deserve you will retrieve.
What you can do,
Because someone is relying on you.
Having faith and don't doubt,
And being happy it's about.

Give Us The Strength

To let go,
And know how and when to say no.
To walk away,
And see a brighter day.
To know when we are truly tired and will do something about it,
And not just continue to deal with it and in our misery sit.
To choose happiness and peace,
And with what or who that has been holding
us back please let us release.
To exhaust everything but if it's still not
working be able to say I'm done,
And come up with a plan and with it run.
To say I've done all I can and know to do,
It's time to enjoy something or someone new.
To be free, and rid ourselves of the burdens, sleepless
nights, stress, and doubts that over takes thee.
In fear not to live,
And what's on your heart and mind say and the truth give.
To go and not look back,
And trust that God will make a way with any lacks.
Not to continue to listen to the lies,
And believe the cries.

That excuses for ourselves and others we have to stop,
And the I, we and they are not perfect we all
already know this so saying this drop.
With that being said fully work on your change,
And things in our lives remove and rearrange.
To know that we can,
And not look at our situation and not
depend on any woman or man.
To stop dealing with and keep doing the same old things,
And embrace what we truly deserve and
let a new beginning spring.
Not to settle for less,
Our worth express.
To give up our worries,
And not to believe in the cry wolf stories.
To know when it's real or fake,
And the right choices and decisions make.
To not cover up but reveal the truth,
And regardless of my age always live out my youth.
To know our limits and length,
It's going to take you God to give us the strength.

Wear Your Shoes

It's a custom fit,
Because it has a destiny to go to every bit.
It's equipped for the journey ahead,
Put them on because only by you they will be led.
Yours are just for your feet,
So, lead and not follow your own journey complete.
Stop judging someone else's pair,
Focus on you and if another is needed ask God
because He is the only one to provide a spare.
Don't worry about if they will be too big or small,
God has already taken care of it all.
In your own stand,
Rather you fall, jump,
leap or hop back on your
feet they will help you land.
So put your own on,
And by no one else should they be worn.
What's for you choose.
And wear your shoes.

Kindness Goes A Long Way

It's about having a heart,
And doing and being there for others is how it starts.
Don't let someone else's frustration and misery affect you,
Overwhelm them with kindness is what you do.
Don't stoop to their level,
And don't give power to the devil.
Always think before you say or do,
Seek God first in everything and ask God is this you.
No matter who does you wrong,
You do what's right and on God's word stand strong.
Your battles pick, and with God's will stick.
For the discomfort, embarrassment, sleepless nights,
aggravation, and stress you will come through,
Just hold on and be patient your blessings you will view.
Don't be nasty, rude,
having an attitude and being controlling as they did,
Always kill them with kindness don't ever
quit and your resentment get rid.
To look the other way, forgive and not
retaliate back can be a big challenge,
But let God be your strength and then you can manage.
The devil tries to defeat you every day,
But know kindness goes a long way.

Shavetta Craig

Not Perfect

Efforts we give,
And producing our all while we live.
Sometimes the same mistakes will be made but not on purpose,
Lessons after lessons then the greatest will surface.
Trust that a person can get it,
It's not for us to quit.
Trials and errors are how we learn,
As trying, doing and being there are how we earn.
Failures will take place,
But success waits to gain its space.
In a person there is so much good,
But others focus so much attention on the bad or wrong and
don't give them the credit and appreciation they should.
Every day won't be great,
But a positive attitude we continue to create.
We continue to hold our heads high,
Even though sometimes we cry.
Focus on what goes right and in timing it will be fixed the wrong,
Everyone has a weakness but a lot of
strength that makes them strong.
Going the extra mile, always being there, helping,
supporting and being very reliable must count
for a lot and should be shown respect,
So, know that things will not always go as planned, the ball
will be dropped, someone will forget or things
can get overwhelming and busy,
so, with that being said we are not perfect.

I Cry

Because I feel and see your pain,
As in any bad or unhealthy situation you can't remain.
Because you deserve better,
Go after your happiness as life awaits you and be that go getter.
Because a change and improvement we all can do,
But we have to know our worth and the power
we hold so that means no settling, fearing,
or doubting as God is waiting for us to make
a move and that means me and you.
Because we get content in our comfort zone,
When a long time ago we should have been gone.
Because we choose to stay with the wrong,
Instead of having confidence and becoming strong.
Because I hate seeing you this way,
That's why for you I constantly pray.
Because my heart feels yours,
But I trust God I know He will open doors.
I will always try,
Because the victory,
healing and good results will come from when I cry.

Go Hard For You

I know soon your happiness you will choose,
Living life is waiting on you there is nothing to lose.
Settling is not the game,
And living in misery is lame.
Fear and doubt you must cast away,
Seek confidence, strength, determination,
and consistency each day.
Want to smile constantly,
Because on you yours looks lovely.
Get back your happy feeling,
And grasp peace and hold on to it and
don't let it go it's your healing.
Your heart is your guide,
All the answers you need is there listen
to it as wisdom it provides.
In all ways I'm going to feed you the truth, real and
knowledge so in your mind it sinks,
Something to always make you think.
You have to be fair,
So do your part to show you care.
What's broke fix it but if it can't be fixed then move on,
It will hurt but day by day they will get over the scorn.
With what makes you happy pick,
And with true love stick.
The right decisions make,
Even if it causes a heartbreak.
Putting you first I know you can and will do,
That's why I go hard for you.

The Truth

It cuts,
And it doesn't need your if, and or buts.
It hurts,
You will be alright so dust off the dirt.
It's a reality check,
It has purpose just like the neck.
It makes you silent,
And no need to get violent.
It must be heard,
Even if you think it's absurd.
From it you can't run,
To receive it, it's not always fun.
It carries a lot of weight,
But it's to make you great.
We don't like to hear it,
But it's much needed every bit.
Can be hard words to swallow,
But it's the best advice to follow.
Will never fail you,
What's best for you it wants you to view.

It brings relief,
To get you out of your grief.
It you push away from,
Just embrace it and to it come.
It will set you free,
So happy you can be.
It's to get you right,
And bring the realness to light.
It's like dwelling in your youth,
You can't go wrong with the truth.

You Have To Learn

To things put an end,
Regardless if they are family or friends.
To stop,
And with things and people how to drop.
How and when to walk away,
And on the situation give it to God and you pray.
To say no,
And when to stay and to go.
To open your eyes,
And don't get caught up in the lies.
Listen to your conscious and use your mind,
And by bad habits don't become blind.
When someone is trying to help,
Let them because they see your pain and hear your yelp.
To have boundaries, and do what's necessary.
Being nice is cool, But know limits and don't be anyone's fool.
Tries cut,
And stop the excuses and the buts.
When enough is enough,
And get balls and speak your mind and be tough.
How to detach,
and don't let the wrong things to you catch.
To get out of your comfort zone and that shell,
And tell whoever and whatever to go to hell.
To not be stubborn and act,
And do what's best for you and make an impact.
How to have a voice,
And know that you have a choice.
To be the hero, umbilical cord, defense, peacemaker,
support line, middle man, and lifeline you yearn,
There is always a time, season, and reason that you have to learn.

Shavetta Craig

Spread Your Wings And Fly

Anything takes effort,
So, meet destiny at its court.
Fear and doubt are in the dictionary,
But don't let it be a part of your vocabulary.
So, get off your knees,
And your purpose seize.
Step into the now it's your moment,
And let your actions be your comment.
Don't hold back just do,
Have faith and confidence in you.
See pass yesterday,
today and search for tomorrow,
So, your dreams follow.
Life's journey explore,
And for yourself want more.
Into your future tap,
And for your finish clap.
To get anywhere from point A to B you must leave,
So, to succeed you must believe.
You won't know the results if you don't try,
So spread your wings and fly.

In Life Things Happen

You never know what it will dish,
You pray for it to be great is your wish.
Wrong, the bad, the ugly,
the hurt and pain and the failure are not what you seek,
But you have to trust your instincts, gut,
and heart when it speaks.
Things in life you just don't choose,
To be unhappy, miserable or in any aspect abuse.
In life we want and deserve the best,
But we will be faced in our lives with many tests.
Unexpectedly and known with those we love we have to
experience or hear about their last breath,
It is a part of life that we must deal with and that's death.
We fall in love and sometimes fall out of it,
We have done all we could but no changes then
the right thing to do is call it quits.
Divorce is not something that you want to do,
But when you have tried and done all you can then you have
to seek the peace and happiness for you.
We sometimes listen to the wrong voice,
Then we have to deal with the choice.
We can heal,
But the past we must peel.
Great and better will follow,
Just have faith in tomorrow.
Just know there is a now and then,
We are unaware because in life things happen.

Shavetta Craig

For All

In life to succeed,
And to meet needs.
To reap rewards,
And ahead move towards.
To come together to produce results,
And no one is perfect we all have faults.
To reach the top,
And dreams don't stop.
Blessings to see,
And humble and faithful to be.
To smile,
And show a gesture by going the extra mile.
To have answered prayers,
To show kindness and cares.
To do what's right,
And with faith don't lose sight.
To love one another as we should,
And do if we could.
To see helping as a duty,
And be positive and not moody.

To someone reach,
And a valuable lesson teach.
To have a giving heart,
And doing your part.
To mature, blossom and grow,
And who Are you know.
In God trust,
Never give up so brush off the dust.
Don't be selfish and be the reason someone else stands tall,
You should want the same for all.

Shavetta Craig

Give Us The Strength

To leave when we should,
After we know we have done all we could.
To know that we have power,
And our current situation we can devour.
To follow our heart,
And it's okay to say that we had enough and we
won't make it to until death do us part.
To speak our mind,
And true happiness find.
To say no,
And not stay but go.
To live and be,
And something greater see.
To take heed to signs,
And with your will get aligned.
To use our heads,
And to rely on God our daily bread.
To know that we can do and have better,
And the storms we will get thru and weather.
To let love show us the way,
And believe and trust in what we pray.
To say goodbye,
And to always try.
To go to all lengths,
To what is needed God please give us the strength.

Walk Away

I know it may be hard,
But let down your guard.
The damage was done,
You finally realize they are not the one.
It's better to see,
Happy I want you to be.
It will now be your old,
Something new cling to and hold.
It won't be your fault,
It's time to see greater results.
Don't worry about others,
Because no more in misery, unhappiness, bored,
not having your own space and not being in love you
don't want to be smothered.
You will be fine,
So, what's next for you, get in line.
It's never too late,
You deserve better so that anticipate.
For you I pray,
Because it's time for you to walk away.

Shavetta Craig

Just Do It

Don't think too long,
Take the initiative and be strong.
Do what you have to do,
And make sure it's right for you.
Get the courage to fulfill that dream,
It's your time to beam.
Stay in your lane and follow your track,
With no excuses and quit holding back.
What you want and deserve reach,
And practice what you preach.
It's not for you to overthink,
Release yourself from the situation or problem in which you sink.
Don't care about what others think or would say,
So, step out on faith today.
A risk is the ability to choose,
The fact that you did something different
and new rather you win or lose.
From the nest fly,
And always continue to try.
You were given wings,
Use them and see what springs.
Just run,
And don't stop until the assignment is done.
It's no time to doubt, fear, worry or quit,
So, leap and just do it.

To Make You Think

If common makes sense,
when are you going to apply it,
Because wisdom and knowledge will
always win it will never quit.
Damage goods make the best creation when they know and
understand their worth again,
As their scars, pain and hurt will mend.
To shine you must glow,
So, turn darkness into colors and your purpose know.
Why keep getting burn by fire,
So, pay attention and choose your desires.
To achieve it you must believe it,
Regardless of the many falls and challenges continue to chase
after your dreams, potentials and goals every bit.
Your future is just like faith before your eyes it can't be seen,
So, your trust in God lean.
Disappointments are the key to make you develop and improve,
You are strong so your mountains tell them to move.
Why do you keep your wrongs, mistakes,
and faults handy and on repeat,
Please sooner than later make it out of your life a delete.
Life has its ways but you are not created to sink,
It's an element to make you think.

It's Time To Be Tired

You have been comfortable for so long but
uncomfortable you need to be,
So, what God has for you get prepared to see.
You did a lot of good, bad, and ugly and you did your dirt,
You had sleepless nights, lied, was lost, confused,
and have done and had your share of hurt.
You complained and grumbled,
But God still carried you even though you still stumbled.
God got you but you still do the same,
You must take life seriously because it's no game.
In the right way, have fun,
And let God's will be done.
You say you are going to change but you remain,
Aren't you weary, don't let this kryptonite
continue to cause you pain.
You go up then you fall back down,
Just choose the righteous way so you can turn your life around.
Please get it together,
So, what's for you can make your life better.
Troubles and struggles aren't supposed to last always,
When doing the same things and keep getting the same
results until you learn you will battle all your days.
Take heed to console and reason,
And watch God work on your behalf in your season.
Get the strength to say self your fired,
And get to the point to say it's time to be tired.

Encouragement Matters

To make it through the day,
That's why we have to pray.
Because we don't have it all together,
But a spoken word can make things better.
When life throws us curve balls,
Jesus is the source to handle it all.
When heavy we feel,
Cast our cares and burdens so we can heal.
To know that we all go through,
As a thank you, comfort, support, you're going
to make it, and don't give up are due.
When challenges begin to pile,
Sometimes all it takes is a simple smile.
When we feel no one cares,
But when we least expect it, someone shows up to be there.
There are days and moments that we need a release,
But right on time from a source here comes peace.
Regardless of our name, title, or position,
We can be guided by our intuition.
With life, pain, hurt, brokenness, and shatters,
It very important to know that encouragement matters.

Shavetta Craig

It's All About

Your test,
Because yet to come is your best.
Being still,
And following God's will.
By faith to walk,
And life talk.
Do you trust,
Because believing in God is a must.
Having hope,
So, for a little while longer with the storm cope.
Holding on,
Because joy will come from the scorn.
Persevering all the way,
And always pray.
Seeking God,
As He is your shield and rod.
Believing that it's going to happen for you,
So, claiming do.
Knowing that God is going to do it,
You can't quit.
Getting over your fear and doubt,
As coming through hardship, trials, challenges, storms,
and troubles to receive the blessings it's all about.

Taken Care Of

Your fears,
And the reason for your tears.
The sleepless nights,
And the things you didn't do right.
That situation that keeps playing in your mind,
And answers to the questions you can't find.
The reasons for your stress,
Cast your cares because you will be bless.
That broken heart,
Mending is a beautiful art.
Your circumstances,
You will win, get back up and have an increase in your finances.
What you can't see,
Faith, trusting and believing must be in thee.
Your strife,
And that thing that's trying to destroy your life.
How you will make it every day,
Timing is everything and you will see the way.
That deadline,
And those thoughts that makes you feel that things won't be fine.
Again, you will love,
Just know whatever you are going thru it's taken care of.

Rise Above It

The pieces may fall,
Let God create something new and again stand tall.
In it don't dwell,
Get the strength again to prevail.
Ashes came from your burn,
But there was a lesson learned.
It's not for you to be down,
Get up from the ground.
It happened yes,
It's history so now make success.
A bad may have provoke,
But to your greatness stay woke.
Look for tomorrow,
Something new and don't dwell into yesterday's sorrows.
The failure made,
Ok the price you paid.
Don't let it make you sink,
Everything happens for a reason so get it together and think.
This is your clean slate,
Come on an elevate.
Up, down, rich, and poor,
You mastered it all so now you know the process on how to soar.
Remember just don't quit,
With whatever you are going thru rise above it.

Happiness Is What I Live For

To make a mend,
And creating smiles as a trend.
To dwell in joy,
So, my peace don't destroy.
To see hearts with love that overwhelms,
And the kindness, delight and care enjoy them.
In life find pleasure,
And the greatest of it treasure.
To be light that shines,
And show compassion each day like it's Valentines.
Laughter keeps things alive,
And positivity thrive.
The key is to be glad,
And to have the best fulfillment ever had.
It's what greets you at every door,
Because happiness is what I live for.

Shavetta Craig

The Beauty Of My Scars

Can you see who I truly am,
A living witness and God's lamb.
I was broken,
But God still knew I was a vital token.
Do I reveal the images of my hurt,
God mold me again from clay and dirt.
I'm not the reflection of my marks,
In others' lives I can still spark.
While enduring pain,
Strength and wisdom I have gained.
Even though I was abused,
Still, me God used.
Jesus endured thirty-two stripes for me,
And great and mighty is He.
You may see a scratch,
But to me the Holy Spirit is attached.
Destruction I had to escape,
But I'm still powerful with my scrapes.
Visual was my burn,
But the sorrow into joy it turns.
I had to flee the matrimony,
Thru it I have a story and testimony.
I still have a glow,
What God has brought me thru you just don't know.
Inside I bleed,
But I'm still available to help another in need.
My smile doesn't really show what I have been thru,
I show and share the goodness and the blessing
of the Lord that I have to you.
The not so pretty can be improved by far,
That's the beauty of my scars.

Keep

God first and the reason why we thrive,
And keep hope, peace, and faith alive.
The chemistry brewing,
And happiness together pursuing.
The fire burning,
And the likeness and desire for each other yearning.
The connection together,
And making and creating life better.
The communication going,
And being there showing.
The love strong,
And the commitment staying long.
The interest there,
And always provide and give a care.
The fulfillment to submitting,
And remaining profound and solid without quitting.
Our word and vow,
And no negativity allow.
The trust forever,
And breaking each other's heart never.
The actions consistent,
And our best being persistent.
The smile to stay,
And the prayers we pray.
The purpose for joy and a sensation to feel,
And always keeping it real.
Each other as the only one,
And let the passion, intimacy, and romance stay
lit and continue to be adventurous and fun.
Building so we can reap,
And the bond, friendship, and relationship
between us let's for a lifetime keep.

From Scratch

It's going to take a shake,
And something to break.
You will have to press,
And pour in more and not less.
To it you will add and measure,
Because it will have treasures.
Stir and mix,
Dash and sprinkle love, joy, peace, wisdom,
mercy, grace, and happiness to the fix.
You will have to drain,
Because thru the process it will gain.
Through it sift,
Examine it carefully this is a mighty gift.
Pull and roll to give it a shape,
The extras can be used by others so don't let it escape.
Get it array,
The time is coming to have it for display.
Place to form and sit,
And you will be proud of the results every bit.
Wait and with timing it will come out right,
This creation will be to the world light.
Great things to it are attached,
As it was molded from scratch.

A Gold Mine With No Dynamite

Are you aware of the treasures in thee,
They need to be birth and discovered so others can see.
You continue to produce,
But this value to the world needs to be introduce.
You are sitting on something great,
Ignite it so others can be blessed, healed, delivered,
and set free from what you create.
With just a peak,
What you have to offer others want to seek.
You have others voicing to you,
Your treasures are building up what are you going to do.
The treasures are in an overflow,
You must explode so to others you can sow.
The treasures go way deep,
Break through so they can leap.
No longer on your treasures can you sit,
It's time to release it.
You carry what others need,
You are the source to plant in them seeds.
What you have don't cover,
Share and around you people will receive and hover.
Why can't you see and believe what others see,
A blessing of worth is thee.
What's in you has to stir,
So amazing things can occur.
Your treasures are supposed to be found,
Because you hold the key to something astound.
It's been peeped the treasures in you,
Pop and blow because it's been long overdue.
Dig, shovel, tear down, pry open, and ignite,
Take heed no more are you a gold mine with no dynamite.

Beginning To End

Things we start we want to see it finish,
Always keep faith and don't let your dreams diminish.
There is a first and a last,
And a future to build and getting over the past.
From A to Z,
There is a process to get to where you want to be.
Thank God for morning and then night,
And being delivered from darkness to see light.
There is always a sunrise and a sunset,
So, in your life God let.
We love birth and dislike death,
Enjoy every moment of life with every breath.
You must crawl before you walk,
And learning to listen before you talk.
Transitioning from sins to righteousness,
So, in life you can have more than less.
In life there is good, challenges, and
changes and in situations to bend,
When we are talking about beginning to end.

Unseen

It's not for you to view,
That's why the impossible and miracles are for God to do.
It's important to remember that God's timing is everything,
What's for you God will bring.
By faith you must walk,
And in what you believe, want to receive,
claim, decree, declare, speak and talk.
This is why unexpectedly, suddenly,
and surprisingly it happens for you,
That's why the sufferings, pain, trials, tribulations,
storms, and troubles you must go through.
It's to get you to comprehend that with God nothing impossible,
As it's for you to know that He is able.
You will never know when, why, how, or where,
Just stay in hope and know you will get there.
Be still and pray is a command,
Just do, it's not for you to understand.
Your trust in God lean,
And watch Him bless you with the unseen.

Release

Prayers will always be said for you,
But the worrying and stressing you can't do.
Yes, it's for you to help and be there for others
but don't carry the heavy burden weight,
So, enjoy peace, life, relaxation, and
happiness before it's too late.
Other people's problems,
It's for them to seek God for Him and not you to solve them.
Pressure comes when carrying someone else's load,
Free yourself and stay on your path and road.
Be careful of who is in your ear and what they say,
And keep your circle small and get with
people who know how to pray.
Those who live in misery, talk too much, always
negative, and who are out to kill, steal, and destroy,
Wise up God created life for you to enjoy.
What is dark,
And let a fire in you again spark.
Leave your past behind,
And the future God has for you find.
Forgiveness to all who has done you wrong,
And let love keep you strong.
So, kill people with kindness,
don't mess up your blessings for anyone, stay positive,
and watch your increase,
So, what does not belong to you please let God and release.

The Signs

You are about to be bless,
That's why you are going through and having
hardships and with you the enemy mess.
See it's up from here,
God is about to show up and show out so the
storms and troubles will disappear.
You are at the end and at your after a while,
As others are about to see your permanent smile.
Just because you came to a stop,
What's for you is not denied,
in God's timing it will drop.
Being still is not a delay,
Thank Him now and get ready because
the blessings are on the way.
God is preparing you so He had to slow you down,
So, get excited about the turn around.
You don't know where you are going,
But ahead cautions God is showing.
So, to position you for the best there was a slight pause,
You are about to manifest and an overflow, increase,
and double portion are attached as well
as the more and just because.
God is not saying no, He will tell you when to go.
So don't get caught up in the wait,
Things for you are about to accelerate.
The things for you are getting align,
So, pay attention to the signs.

With Interest

What was on hold,
An abundance from it is going to unfold.
For all the lacks,
Multiplying and double you are about to get back.
Remember this, the longer the wait,
It adds up and the blessings are going to be great.
It's building up while you are still and you sit,
You are about to gain your profit.
Everything is getting right for you to earn,
You are about to receive a prosperous return.
What's for you, no one can touch,
As the dividends are going to be very much.
In all type of ways, you are going to be paid,
Because it's for you to win and the troubles will fade.
The reaping is about to be at its best,
And you will see God work on your behalf and with interest.

Decreeing And Declaring

That a shift is in the atmosphere,
And miracles will happen everywhere.
That the situation won't remain the same,
Because increase and overflow are calling your and my name.
I will manifest, and it's coming, the best.
That the impossible will take place,
And the winning season and new beginnings embrace.
That this is the year and beyond that the blessings will stack,
And there will be no more lacks.
What I believe, receive, claim, hope, and speak I will view,
And I pray the same over you.
That God is about to blow my mind,
Because prosperity and reaping on me you will find.
It's my rise now,
Because what the enemy was blocking the release God will allow.
It's my turn, I waited, prayed,
remained humble and faithful,
So, the time had come for me to earn.
That what I could never imagine to occur for me,
Nothing is too hard for my God because just that I'm about to see.
And my testimony I will be sharing,
That my God did it unusual, uncommonly,
suddenly, unexpectedly,
and surprisingly I'm decreeing and declaring.

May

God's will you keep,
And the blessings reap.
Doors continue to open for you,
And the impossible watch God do.
You receive a downpour,
And get what you prayed and asked for and more.
Each day you experience a break,
Because it's your time to prosper, to get back,
and increase and it's not a mistake.
God reveal to you His plan, purpose, and ways,
And He is doing it in all 31 days.
Your life turn for the better,
For all the years of the storms, tarry, sufferings,
trials, tribulations, mistakes, lessons, troubles,
and waits you had to weather.
The favor of God on you stay attach,
And the overflow latch.
Is only hours away,
So, get ready for the consecutive wins in the month of May.

God Is Doing It For You

Faith is the most important thing,
Having it is how the miracles and the
impossible God does and brings.
From generations, centuries, decades,
and years God is still the same,
And even now He will do it for you,
He hasn't forgotten you He knows your name.
Yesterday, today, and forever He will make a way,
So, continue to be still, wait, trust, and pray.
Some examples I will give,
So, you won't give up and quit and by faith live.
God is the only help and need for you,
As in His timing He will see you through.
Like Daniel, He protected him from the lions in the den,
So, your day is coming don't worry about the when.
With the woman He stopped her issue with blood,
What's for you is going to pour and flow like a flood.
For Moses He departed the Red Sea,
Just wait your turn the blessings are for thee.
Like Sarah in her old age a child she birthed,
The favor of God is on you,
watch and see while others will see your worth.

A Lazarus was raised from the dead,
You are coming out because by a Mighty God you are led.
As for Peter He opened the prison's doors,
Get ready because this is your winning season
and the year of so much more.
Just like God used and saved Jonah from the whale,
He is looking for you to forgive, repent, cry for help,
and give Him praise, so in your life He can prevail.
Nothing is impossible for God to do,
So don't doubt just have faith because God is doing it for you.

Not Exempt

From what God is doing in this season,
Everything happens for a reason.
From the blessings on the way,
That's the reason why I pray.
Because longer I had to wait,
To be still is how I receive the best and great.
Nor will I be denied,
As I will have joy from the tears I cried.
Because it's happening for me,
See, favor is my destiny.
From God's glory,
Because others will be blessed from my story.
For what's for me to have,
And at the enemy I will laugh.
I am meant to be bless,
Regardless of the struggle, trouble, and mess.
To the setbacks, stumbling blocks, failures,
and negative attempts,
My victory day is coming, so I am not exempt.

The Year Of Restore

The time has come to get back,
You will be rewarded for your lacks.
Because of yourself you gave, you will now get,
So, what was lost, stolen, taken, destroyed,
and broken you will regain every bit.
It's time for you to get back on your feet,
The process God is doing in your life is not complete.
Because you didn't quit,
The blessings be expecting it.
You may be empty but God is going to replenish,
So don't let your faith diminish.
A pour keeps ringing,
Thank you God, and God did it you continue saying and singing.
The back then God is going to replace,
You had to go through to now receive His favor and grace.
Don't worry about the old welcome and embrace the new,
You waited patiently for this God is doing it for you.
God is about to exceed your expectations
with abundance and more,
Because this is the year of restore.

If It Was Easy

To have faith you wouldn't know how to do,
And to see how God works for you.
The struggle wouldn't be real,
And you wouldn't have the strength and willpower to heal.
It wouldn't have been no Jesus, cross, nails, blood, or death,
And it wouldn't be life and you wouldn't have breath.
The impossible and miracles wouldn't exist,
And you wouldn't experience the Holy Spirit in your mist.
The troubles and mistakes wouldn't make you who you are,
And you wouldn't have the determination to move on and go far.
Pain wouldn't be felt,
And you wouldn't know the strength and power
you have to overcome problems to you dealt.
Then you wouldn't understand the trials, tribulations,
and storms you had to go through,
Because after a while, the end, the cease, the tarry,
and the wait there are blessings for you.
There wouldn't be a process,
And you wouldn't know what it would be like to be bless.
How would you discover and know your true worth,
And your gifts and talents wouldn't birth.

You wouldn't know what persevering and
going through is truly about,
And how to not worry, fear, stress, or doubt.
You wouldn't appreciate all that you have,
And know how to live, love, and laugh.
You wouldn't get the concept of happiness, peace, and joy,
Because in an instant everything you would destroy.
Hope couldn't do its part,
And love the most important thing wouldn't know how,
why, where, and when to start.
Something handed and given would defeat the purpose,
So, to earn, yearn, fight, appreciate, value, be worth it, to win,
soar, elevate, sweat, cry, and work hard for had to surface.
Deserving comes with a price,
So, you too have to be a sacrifice.
Life would be a mess, worthless, non-efficient
and incapable if hardship wasn't
a part of thee,
So, what if it was easy?

I Want To Be Rich

In abundance of love to forever sustain,
And with peace in my life to remain.
With joy for a lifetime,
And having a giving heart that makes someone else's heart chime.
In wisdom and knowledge,
And being able to send so many students to college.
In a positive personality,
And the favor and blessings that are on me.
In my smile that I give,
And in happiness live.
In my light the glows, illuminates, and shines,
And in what I can do to make someone else's life fine.
With the prayers that I pray,
And making someone else's day.
In the words that I speak,
And my inspiration, encouragement, comfort,
and support that peek.
Into winning is the switch,
As in worth, value, virtue,
and genuineness I want to be rich.

Shavetta Craig

Don't Let

The enemy disrupt your peace, happiness, and joy,
Because he is out to kill, steal, and destroy.
The enemy invade your space,
Know you have power, favor, and grace.
The enemy get the best of you,
So, pray, plead the blood of Jesus,
know that you are strengthen, have faith, and trust God do.
The enemy convince you that through your storms,
troubles, tests, trials and tribulations,
and sufferings that you have lost,
Just trust and believe God is bringing you
out and the enemy will pay the cost.
The enemy bring you down, feel like there's no way,
or in life problems and situations you are to be mistreated,
Let him know that he is defeated.
The enemy get you caught up in what you see,
Because bless you are going to be.
The enemy mess with your heart and mind,
What was promised in God's word find.
The enemy make you think it's not happening for you
because you feel denied or because of the delay,
God's timing, plan, and the wait are a part of the process,
so just be still and know that God is making a way.
You serve an almighty, awesome, and powerful God, that
protects, provides, redeems, and loves you don't forget,
So, what the enemy is out to do, don't let.

On Purpose

Have a great day,
And for others pray.
Network and connect,
Because we all can learn from someone because we are not perfect.
Make someone else smile,
And do an act of kindness and go the extra mile.
Let your light shine,
And let your future know it will be fine.
Show them what you are made and capable of,
And demonstrate the real and true meaning of love.
Stay committed to your dream,
And know it takes a village and team.
Show that you are going to win,
Because you have gifts and talents within.
Finish what you started,
And from your goals don't be departed.
Prove them wrong,
Because you can do this, you were built to be strong.
Let your tenacity, willpower, determination, and
confidence surface,
And be you on purpose.

Shavetta Craig

Bloom

The seeds are planted,
Gods will be granted.
You have been through a drought,
Now the living waters are about to make you sprout.
You may have withered, dried up,
and didn't bear good fruit,
But a change has come for you to flourish and nourish at the root.
You became frail,
But it's your time to prevail.
You will fertilize,
And you will not be overlooked; You will be recognized.
Your season is next in line,
You have the light to shine.
This time you will grow,
You are beautiful you know.
Out with the old in with the new, so make room,
Because it's time for you to bloom.

Let Nobody

Come before or between you and God,
Because He is your everything and shield and rod.
Steal your joy,
So, the negativity destroy.
Make you feel less,
Because you have come too far so it's for you to be bless.
Stop you from fulfilling your purpose and dream,
Because faith, hope, love, and winning are on your team.
Stand in your way,
Be determined, willing, confident,
and ready every day.
Mistreat you,
Kill them with kindness is what you do.
Tamper with your good,
And love, pray, and encourage as you should.
God is always on time never tardy,
To persuade or convince you differently let nobody.

Shavetta Craig

All Of Me

Is your request,
I will give you my best.
No holding back,
Because with you I have no lacks.
Is my gift,
As in my life you made a shift.
I surrender at your feet,
As it's you that makes me complete.
Please take,
And never leave me nor forsake.
Needs to be touched by you,
So, I can be a creation of a virtue.
To you I submit,
And to your will and ways I commit.
As it's you that I want to see,
God, here is all of me.

I Love You

It's not said much,
These are powerful words that can touch.
It is required indeed,
And it is a need.
It's something that should be felt,
And we have to be careful on how it's dealt.
Don't let it be too late,
So, say and show it now don't wait.
Nothing is not promised tomorrow,
So spread love now and not after sorrow.
It brings joy to your heart,
So today start.
It holds so much weight,
And a smile it creates.
Continue to say it again and again,
It's for family and your friends.
Watch what it will do,
So, know I love you.

Milestone

It wasn't easy to wait,
Because life from here on out is going to be great.
I persevere through the process,
Now it's my turn and time to be bless.
The storms, sufferings, trials, tribulations, troubles,
challenges, and mistakes have taught me a lot,
As faith and hope got me to this spot.
So many years have stacked,
What I have prayed for I will get and receive all I have lacked.
To trust God I learned to accomplish,
Because with me He is not finished.
Timing is everything,
When I was ready God made it happen,
thank God I stayed in the ring.
It paid off for me,
And God did it,
I give Him all the glory.
Even though it took a while,
God was silent, and it seemed like I was alone,
There is nothing too hard for my God,
I made it through this milestone.

Like A Waterfall

Are how my blessings will flow,
As my territory will consistently grow.
The favor on me will always continue,
And being fruitful will be my venue.
The miracles will be like a downpour,
And this is just the beginning,
it's going to be more.
What's for me will never cease,
It's on me to increase.
I will shower into others too,
What God does and did for me I want
Him to do the same for you.
In what's for me I will drench,
And in more than enough I will quench.
I will rise,
And I will always receive suddenly,
unexpectedly, and by surprise.
For everything I'm going to get back all,
Because what was stored up for me is
going to be like a waterfall.

Don't Confuse The Ships

There is a friendship and a relationship,
As there is a difference between the two so don't trip.
It's either a mutual understanding or a vow,
So, making it complicated please don't allow.
Something casual or something to commit,
You are free or to something solid you summit.
You either married or you are single,
Which means you are off the market or you are still able to mingle.
With one it's easy to leave and with the other it's not,
So, if you are not happy,
being treated right,
keep going through the same things,
and putting up with unnecessary stress,
give someone else the opportunity to fill that voided spot.
So, choose wise,
So later you won't be surprised.
It's either like or love,
And we cool or it's you I'm always thinking of.
Be watchful and mindful and be on guard,
Because dating these days is hard.
It can be mutual or a bond,
So don't mix up the two is the tip,
So, friend and relation don't confuse the ships.

Stop Looking For Perfect

You just might miss out,
On something good because you doubt.
Don't get caught up in what you don't see,
Because the best part is within thee.
There will be good and bad,
And a past we all had.
Chances are always given,
As changes are the identity and ways for living.
Meet where they are at,
The growth, building, creating,
and establishing they need that.
A mess can create a beautiful picture,
So, embrace the beauty of the fixture.
Flaws we all have,
So, take the time to learn, discover, get to know, and laugh.
On the care, kindness, and personality reflect,
And stop looking for perfect.

Shavetta Craig

A Gem

They are a hidden treasure,
And is blessed with so much pleasure.
Unique and rare,
And they are all about actions and genuinely love and care.
A precious delight,
When discovered they are a great insight.
With a heart of gold,
A wonderful and sensational person mold.
Lights up a room and is very special too,
And they have a way about them that will mesmerize you.
They say and do things that stays on your
mind and keeps your attention,
They think outside the box,
they are one of a kind,
and they have a beautiful intellect to mention.
Their beauty is defined,
They were made and created differently with a
personality to captivate and blow your mind.
Hold on when you find them,
That exceptional person that is a gem.

Nothing Is

Greater than my being,
What I can do for you and all are worth the seeing.
Impossible for me,
So let my way and will be.
Too hard for me to do,
Because I'm the only one that can see you through.
By me not seen,
So, I have the power to deliver, heal, set free, and make you clean.
Better than my love,
Because what's best and good for you I'm always thinking of.
More important than putting me first,
So, after my word seek and thirst.
Difficult when in me you believe,
That when you have faith to receive.
I have said you are mine and I desire you to say I am His,
So, because of this, me, your God nothing is.

Coming Together

With the turbulence that you face,
Your winning season you are about to embrace.
All the hell you went through,
Miracles, the impossible, and blessings
are about to happen for you.
The wait that you saw as a delay,
The fruitfulness, double portion, victory,
and harvest are on the way.
The pain and hurt that you had to endure,
The best is coming your way for sure.
The scars that have a meaning for each one,
Don't worry because with you God is not done.
The purpose to be still,
Because it's for you to stay focus on God's will.
The why, how, where, and when,
Don't get caught up in all that because what God is
going to do now, He did the same back then.
The reasons for the happening of everything,
As unexpectedly favor to you God will bring.
The storms that occur,
Right before men God will increase her.
You went through the pressure, plucking, pruning, plunging,
positioning, promoting, preparing, and the rain,
But the test was all about in your faith,
trust, and hope in God remain.
Now the time is right for it to happen, things will get better,
Thank you, God, as things are coming together.

Watch God And Not Man

Who do you trust,
I trust and believe in the one who created heaven
and earth and made us from dust.
Who wakes you up every day,
And who do you go to when you pray.
Who loves you more than anything,
And peace, joy, grace, mercy,
happiness, glory to you He brings.
Who will never leave nor forsake you,
And the impossible and miracles only He alone can do.
Who will never let you down,
And in any situation turn it around.
Who is more than enough and able,
And provide you will a roof over your head,
clothes on your back, shoes on your feet,
and food on your table.
Who is always in your court,
And will have the final say and can
change the results of any report.
Who is mighty and great,
And rewards you when He tells you to be still and wait.
Who will not harm you but prosper you with His plan,
So watch God and not man.

Oh Happy Day

You endured so much,
It's now your turn to see God move in your life and be touch.
God will dry those tears up,
And favor and blessings will run over in your cup.
Prepare to smile permanently again,
Because it's your time to mend.
You waited and prayed consistently,
Well, the time is right so the miracles you will see.
It's a reason all unbearable, burdens,
heaviness, and tests happened to you,
Because of your faith and trust in God He is about to
show you and others what He can and will do.
So get ready to thank Him and praise,
Because God is about to show up and show
out in your life in many ways.
The timing is near when you will say,
Oh happy day.

Just Like That

With a snap it will come forth,
As the wait reveals its worth.
With a blink it will appear,
So trust and do not fear.
With a word,
Because your prayers God heard.
With a clap it is yours,
God is opening doors.
With a stump things will tremble,
Because your praise is a sound symbol.
When you move,
What God can do He will prove.
With eyes close and your mouth speaks,
The miracles will start to peak.
Your name is already in the atmosphere and chat,
So it will happen just like that.

Shavetta Craig

Your Faith Keep

The journey will not be easy but the reward will be great,
God has something in store for you so get ready and anticipate.
Don't let discouragement sink in,
Because you will win.
I know it gets unbearable,
But remember God is able.
Just don't lose your mind,
What's for you be still, you it will find.
Life and challenges can be overwhelming,
But soon the blessings you will be welcoming.
Even when you don't know if you are coming or going,
Stay strong and you will manifest keep knowing.
In unbelief, doubt, failures, and loses don't sink,
Just trust in God because your situation can change in a blink.
From the tarry, prolong, wait,
and delay you will reap,
So your faith keep.

Let Us Go

To the house of the Lord,
And worship and be on one accord.
To the mountain top,
And in our faith don't stop.
With God's plan,
Because we can't trust in man.
To give God praise,
And be thankful, grateful, faithful,
and humble all our days.
Into His dwelling place,
As He fills us with His grace.
Over to the other side,
Because only God alone can provide.
See what the Lord has done,
Because we are favored by the Mighty One.
On our knees and let the spirit flow,
Higher let us go.

Shavetta Craig

It's Time

I prepared for this moment,
To see God work in my life with the blessings sent.
God is about to reveal to me what the wait was for,
As 2024 and beyond is the year of open doors,
the pour, and to receive more.
I had to go through the process to bloom,
Now God is about to exceed my expectations
so I have to make room.
I'm ready for what God has for me,
My manifest I will see.
The trials, tribulations, troubles, storms, sufferings,
and tarry will stop, cease, and halt,
I will see the goodness and the overflow, increase,
favor, impossible, and miracles will be my results.
All that I went through served its purpose,
As what's for me will now surface.
I didn't think it would happen for me or take place,
But I had to learn to trust God, be still, wait,
and have faith and I will see God's grace.
So it wasn't a denial, delay, punishment, or opportunity missed,
I had to be planted, positioned,
and promoted for a time like this.
The timing had to be right,
For God to put me in the spotlight.
It's been a long time coming,
but God waited until my prime,
It was worth it, as He says you are ready and it's time.

To Be Light

On others it's for me to shine,
And be what they need to make their life fine.
Every day God let me have on my glow,
So through me you show.
My brightness to others calls,
As I give my all.
I want to be what people need,
And to make them smile and happy indeed.
To illuminate is what I do,
Because my purpose and assignment are to inspire,
encourage, comfort, motivate, support, and to love you.
For others I will always pray,
And be their sunshine ray.
I will let my gift take its course,
As my kindness, hugs, smile, love, gentleness, joy, energy,
and humbleness are my power source.
I'm not perfect but with what you gifted me
with God let me use it to do right,
Because I was created for others to be light.

The Red That Won't Come Out

It's the thing to keep,
Because of it is how you reap.
It's like a stain,
Forever in your life you want it to remain.
It's what makes you pure,
And washes away sins for sure.
It's with you wherever you go,
And like a river it flows.
It keeps you sane,
And heals your pain.
You can be addicted to it,
And will be grateful for it every bit.
It shows,
And helps you grow.
It is your light,
And in you it shines bright.
It's your lifeline,
And it has its way to make you fine.
I'm talking about Jesus' blood,
That protects, renews,
and purifies and flows like a flood.
The price He paid is what I'm talking about,
The red that won't come out.

Only If You Knew

How great God is,
And He is mine and I'm His.
He is the one to see you pass your strife,
And grant you a better life.
The struggles and situations He brought me out of,
Now that is love.
The many tears I cry,
But God still allows me to hold my head up high.
His goodness kept me,
Because from bondage I'm free.
This awesome God that we serve,
What He does for us we don't deserve.
All the harm I faced,
But what saw me thru was God's grace.
It was hard to make it some days,
But I still gave God praise.
That giving up and death came for me,
But God had another plan; He had an assignment for me to see.
All things that God has brought me thru,
Only if you knew.

I Get To

My God and others serve,
And live a life I don't deserve.
With family get close,
And cherish what we have the most.
Show and share love more,
As being together I adore.
Make the best of life,
And just be grateful, humble,
and thankful without the strife.
Enjoy seeing my family laughter and smiles,
And that it stays and continues for miles.
Take the time to be still and learn,
Things about myself and my family to yearn.
Get up each day, and create peace, happiness,
and joy along the way.
Think about and understand what God wants me to see,
And how important coming together,
reconciling, loving, forgiving, listening,
and thriving are to Him, my family and me.
Step back and reevaluate,
And this time something meaningful and awesome create.
See change involved, and problems solved.
Fulfill the things that I miss, and know that I can do this.
Where I have failed an opportunity to get it right and do,
As I get to.

Do You Know He Is Able

He makes life stable,
He is always on time and available.
His word is believable,
He will speak back; He is sociable.
He can make your life changeable,
In your distress He will make you comfortable.
For your actions He will hold you accountable,
He gives a love that is remarkable.
What He did for us is memorable,
Me and He are inseparable.
He is a King that is suitable,
Strength and power to you He will enable.
He can do the impossible and the imaginable,
What He does for us is immeasurable.
He is so loveable,
Use and learn His word it's knowledgeable.
With His will you will not be incapable,
For your sins you are liable.
When trials, tribulations,
and storms are with you at the table,
Don't you know He is able?

That's Sexy

To put God first in his day,
Even though he knows that he is not perfect,
he knows God is the only way.
While still in bed, on his knees, or walking,
To God he is talking.
His time to God he devotes,
And he has spiritual readings and uplifting quotes.
To God he consults,
To show him for himself and that woman
how to produce positive results.
To know that he is covered by God's grace,
He is ready for what he might face.
That in God he trusts,
And having God is a must.
The power of prayer is a great quality for a man to have,
As a woman admires that as he also knows
how to live, love, and laugh.
To know that he will pray for her and with her
is an attraction for a woman to see,
To a woman about a man, that's sexy.

From Me

From my rib she came,
And he, she, man, and woman, she even has a part of my name.
To me she is a major effect,
Even though neither one of us is perfect.
To care for her because she is mine,
Because she is worthy and divine.
We are two but are truly one,
As she will bear my daughter or son.
She is the best part,
That's why she has a way about herself to captivate my heart.
I am proud and honored to walk beside her,
As my smile and your glow others can view,
so watch out there now, she is mine sir.
She holds a power to make me do anything,
As so much joy, peace, structure, meaning,
and understanding to me she brings.
God created her because she was necessary,
And for me to love her very.
I am so very grateful and thankful for you,
Because you are an amazing creation and great at what you do.
To keep her happy, loved, protected, provided for, adored,
and treasured it's for me to do it and to see,
As a beautiful, virtuous, and unique creation a woman is from me.

Period

God makes a way and is the only way,
And wakes me up each and every day.
Gods will be done,
And I trust and believe in Him the only One.
Prayer really does changes things,
As the impossible and miracles God brings.
God is real,
As by an ask, touch, or request He heals.
God can make anything shift, turn around, and move,
Through me He is going to prove.
God will show and give reasons that He is the I Am and Savior,
And He loves me that's why He grants me favor.
With faith I believe that God is,
And to reward and bless me the timing is His.
From Genesis to Revelation,
His word will not come void and He will exceed my expectations.
Hope is my proof,
Because He will do it for me as He did for the lady with the issue
of blood and the man that was lowered down through the roof.
From my mouth all you would hear is God did it,
Because only He can period.

Change

Just like the time on the clock,
What's for me no one can block.
Just like the seasons,
It happens for many reasons.
Just like the days of the week,
Blessings after blessings I will seek.
Just like a name,
I wasn't meant to be the same.
From day to night,
Things may have started out dark but it will become bright.
The position,
Because it's time to transition.
The mentality of how it use to be,
And something greater and better see.
It's not impossible to do,
It's waiting for a new view.
Even if it seems strange,
It's a wonderful thing, it's coming, and it's
working for me, I'm talking about change.

Jesus

It has a good ring,
And great things He brings.
It's the name to call,
Because for us He gave His all.
I love Him,
He brought light to the dim.
When it's mentioned,
It gets everybody's attention.
Is the way,
And He is the guidance every day.
Is the one to deliver,
He gives you a quiver.
Who is Master and Savior,
And grants favor.
Who we call friend,
And time in His presence spend.
He is everything to us,
Let's hear it for Jesus.

There's Still

Miracles to take place,
And to seek mercy and grace.
Repentance and forgiveness to do,
Because God still wants to use you.
Time to change,
And better a relationship that is estrange.
A reason to hope,
So continue to cope.
A future to live,
And much to give.
In you much breath,
So serve your purpose until death.
Something to live for,
And for you God has so much more.
Love to sustain,
And joy, happiness, and peace to gain.
A chance to follow God's will,
Because a plan for you there's still.

Shavetta Craig

God Is So Good

Because He gave me life,
And delivers me from sin and strife.
As He wakes me up every day,
And He hears when I pray.
He is the best Father and friend ever,
And He lets me down never.
Life is better with Him,
And He is light to the dim.
He directs my path,
And I see how great He is from the aftermath.
Because without Him possible nothing would be,
And in many ways blessings I continue to see.
He has brought me through so much stuff,
He is more than enough.
I thank Him and praise Him as I should,
So trust me when I say God is so good.

Wait For It

To receive the blessings that may take long,
But in your faith stay strong.
As it tarries to harvest it will do,
Because God is doing the impossible for you.
The vision will manifest at the appointed hour,
And watch God suddenly have an overflow on you shower.
The love that is meant to be,
As a lifetime with the one for you God will let you see.
To go up in your season,
But you had to suffer a while, be tested, mature,
and learn lessons are the reasons.
The answers to your prayers,
God got you because for you He cares.
The unexpected and suddenly that will take place,
Because the unexplainable and increase that God did,
you are going to embrace.
That smile that has been waiting a while to beam,
And how God exceed your expectations more
than you can imagine or dream.
The desires of your heart,
Timing is everything it will do its part.
Patience and perseverance will pay off so don't quit,
So the miracles wait for it.

Shavetta Craig

Is There

A problem too difficult,
For God not to deliver great results.
Something too hard for Him to do,
Or a trial that He didn't bring you through.
A miracle that He couldn't perform,
Or didn't see you out of a storm.
Nothing He can't get you out of,
Or that He never showed you love.
A time you, He will leave or forsake,
Or didn't forgive you of your sins and mistakes.
A moment He never was on time or good,
Or not answer your prayers as He could.
A promise that He didn't keep,
And the impossible can He not do for you to reap.
A day that you couldn't count on Him,
Or can He not do for you now what He did back then for them.
Anything He can't see,
Or make it happen for thee.
A reason that He is not everywhere,
Anything that God can't handle, is there?

Are You Ready

For the manifest,
Because you endured the storms, troubles,
and tribulations from the test.
To go to the next level,
It was challenging but you didn't give in to the devil.
To see what God had for you,
Because giving up you didn't do.
To go up, higher, and climb,
Because it's your time.
For your great,
As it wasn't easy but you continued to wait.
For the miracles and the impossible you were being still for,
Because God is about to provide blessings,
overflow, double portions, increase, and so much more.
To see the reason,
Why God stretched and prolonged your winning season.
Because the time is now because you remained steady,
The reveal is happening so are you ready?

Shavetta Craig

At The Altar

I lay,
And confess, intercede, and pray.
I cast my cares and burdens,
And my soul and spirit opens.
I surrender my all,
As an anointing on me fall.
My heart cries,
As what's been trying to take me out dies.
I will kneel,
And will be healed.
You will have my attention,
As the name of Jesus,
I continue to mention.
I have a release,
And I receive the needed peace.
Is a comfort place,
And I'm covered by grace.
Others come too,
To accept what you are going to do.
A change will occur,
God as I meet you at the altar.

God Is Going To Show Up

Just like a creep,
Unexpectedly you are going to reap.
Like a shadow of doubt,
God is showing out.
Don't let the distance and silence deter you,
In the right timing watch what God will do.
In the impossible believe,
Because by faith you will receive.
Continue to have hope in what you prayed for,
Because God will see it come to pass and soar.
God is saying get it,
Because it's for you to go through but the
solution is not to quit.
Do you want it bad,
Even if it does happen right away will you
continue to wait and still be glad.
When you are not expecting,
That's when God starts intercepting.
It may be empty now but God is filling up your cup,
Because God is going to show up.

Faith

Don't lose,
And your blessings chose.
Walk by,
And on God rely.
Continue to trust in,
Because it's for you to win.
Is the hope that you need,
To manifest indeed.
Is about seeing the impossible take place,
And miracles to embrace.
In you God wants to see,
As proud He will be.
Is the only way,
So dwell in it every day.
Is your guide,
And watch God provide.
It's to believe in what God had saith,
So have faith.

I Will Do It

It's not going to be easy but it's the only way,
And to begin I will pray.
Trust when it seems impossible to,
Because God will see me through.
Wait until the time is right,
So when it's supposed to happen God will give me the invite.
Having faith is the only way to see,
And it shall and will manifest for me.
Forgive when it's difficult,
Even though it will take time to get over the hurt,
brokenness, and the insult.
Believe that God can do all things,
Even in my storms, tribulations, troubles, and sufferings.
Give glory in my pain,
Faithful to God I must remain.
Be for others a need,
And until they harvest continue to water my mustard seeds.
Heal from the scars that are my witness,
And knowing that God will see me through this.
Persevere, push, press, and praise while in the pit,
So for God, I will do it.

Silently

For help you cry,
Because with every situation you continue to try.
You hide your pain,
And you are doing everything to stay sane.
You question what you are doing,
As many choices and decisions you are pursuing.
You want to give up,
Because so many storms, challenges, obstacles,
and problems filling up your cup.
You feel life's pressure,
As peace, joy,
and happiness you want to endure.
You don't know what to do,
As to your self-worth you want to be true.
You just want someone to hold your hand,
And love have and understand.
You are asking for things to get better,
Because so many battles you weather.
You are trying to catch a break,
And learn from your mistakes.
You are trying to breathe,
And to something fulfilling cleave.
You feel depressed and have anxiety,
But you still smile as you are suffering
through these things silently.

When You Are Losing

Your grip to God's hand,
Because what you are going through you don't understand.
Your belief in those around you, including family and friends too,
Because they are not proving what they claim they would do.
Your faith to see it manifest,
No one said it would be easy to endure the test.
Your patience to wait,
Because it's taking long what you anticipate.
Your hope in something that you asked and prayed for,
As the enemy keeps saying you don't deserve it so
don't look for a pour, more, or that open door.
To the temptation that you don't want or need to go back to,
As it keeps calling and saying the wrong never deceived you.
Because you are overtaken by fear and doubt,
Continue to persevere it won't run out.
The enemy keeps playing with your mind,
So the scriptures that holds all power find.
Just hold on and God keep choosing,
And trust God and His timing when you are losing.

Shavetta Craig

For Your Labor

Your hard work will not be in vain,
When the time is right you will gain.
And all you have been through will not go unnoticed,
Just know that miracles are coming after this.
It was heard the many times you weep,
As joy and happiness, you will reap.
Kept going when it was so hard to,
But your faith will let you receive blessings due to you.
Suffered when others couldn't see,
You will be the evidence of the impossible to be.
When hearing it's not going to happen, you're crazy,
give up, it couldn't have been me, you don't deserve it,
You could do better, and other negative insults,
For trusting God double portion, increase, fruitfulness,
and an overflow will be your results.
You continue to persevere and sweat,
So God's will and your desires you will get.
Troubles stir,
But God's plan will occur.
You will be granted favor,
For your labor.

Don't Let Your Past

Dictate your future,
So heal and the right one will come along to be the suture.
Stop you from loving again,
In time you will mend.
Make you bitter,
And with possibilities don't be a quitter.
Scar you permanently,
Because there are better potentials to see.
Hold you hostage,
So let starting over be a privilege.
Get you out of character,
Regardless of how much it was a disaster.
Harden your heart,
Forgiving and move on is a start.
Make you negative,
So learn and continue to live.
Bad and trouble won't always last,
So becoming heartless, don't let your past.

Just Do It

It's not an easy task,
But in faith you must bask.
You get anxious when what you prayed for is not fulfill,
It's all about being still.
It's a process as timing is the bait,
So learn to wait.
Get back up and move,
It will happen God will prove.
Quitting and giving up is not the way,
It's to dwell in hope each day.
Through the journey hardships and challenges you will endure,
But you must trust for sure.
Even when it wasn't so good to you,
Loving continue to do.
Believe in God every bit,
Even when it's difficult just do it.

In Advance

For the blessings I will prepare,
Because to my destiny I will reach there.
God, I'm thanking you,
Because of you a brighter future I will view.
I'm getting ready for what's for me,
Because I waited and was patient to meet my destiny.
I will rejoice,
Because God you will always be my choice.
I will get in position,
As my life is in transition.
I will let faith be my guide,
Because God will provide.
All glory, praise, honor,
and love God to you belong,
Because when the time is right it will
happen for me and won't prolong.
God will see me through any circumstance,
So God, I'm praising you in advance.

Shavetta Craig

Be Salt

Like a major part,
Just like the heart.
Bring seasoning to the mix,
As it's the essential to fix.
An added substance,
And a wanted resistance.
To serve a purpose or need,
And souls feed.
Not to have too much of but just a pinch to make it right,
And for a reason it will be a delight.
A flavor,
That hits the spot to savor.
An inquired preservative,
And a long time additive.
To give taste,
And meaningful in many ways with nothing to waste.
Be useful like the ingredient malt,
And in someone's life be salt.

A Human Being

Perfect we are not created to be,
But our sins, mistakes, failures,
and falls will get us to our destiny.
In good ways it's for us to grow,
And God know.
A living vessel,
As with life we wrestle.
Different emotions we feel,
And we hurt and we heal.
We go through bleeds,
But God wants us to make Him a need.
What transpires in life we are equipped to handle,
As God is our mantel.
We rise and we fall,
But we try again and stand tall.
We lose and we win,
And we can choose to do right or sin.
Uniquely and wonderfully made,
With love within us to never fade.
It's more to us than the seeing,
The life of a human being.

Shavetta Craig

I Count It All Joy

My best was saved for last,
Because my future is looking greater than my past.
My lacks were just a set up for my increase,
And added to me was happiness, love, and peace.
To wait was the gift,
As blessings in my direction shift.
The pain, hurt, scars, and brokenness to endure,
I will reap a harvest for sure.
The many tears I have cried,
I'm winning now because suffering, trials,
drought, and tarry has died.
With everything I have been through,
I'm ready because the impossible God is about to do.
The hell that tried to remain,
But it failed because favor is on my life, it's for me to gain.
The sleepless nights,
But I got rest because what God has for me is a delight.
Struggling the way that I did,
But when I started walking by faith; fear,
worry, doubt, and stress hid.
God is giving me back what the enemy killed and destroyed,
It's my time as I count it all joy.

Let It Rain

A flood great,
As the overflow you anticipate.
To help the seed grow,
So prepare for the harvest that you sow.
To make things mold,
Like mud and clay to create an image to unfold.
To make clean,
Something profound that has never been seen.
Because water is needed as half and more
of the human body is made of,
It's just like love.
The shower down keep,
As it's our way to reap.
As through the storms,
With faith that's how miracles and blessings are formed.
As on it Jesus walked,
So listen when He talks.
In life it takes waiting, trusting, saturating,
and processing to gain,
So God let it rain.

Learn

To let go when you should,
And choose what and the one for you that is good.
To release your past and move on,
And in time you will heal and get over your scorn.
To take heed to what God is trying to tell and show you,
It's what He wants and not what you want to do.
To take risks and give that person or thing a chance,
This could be your true opportunity for success,
happiness, love, and romance.
To put God first and always pray,
And let Him guide you every day.
To trust your instincts,
And positive thoughts think.
To make time,
Everything is not all about making a dime.
To forgive, and life live.
To laugh more, and love galore.
To be consistent, and continue to be persistent.
To choose faith over fear,
Because things are not always what they appear.
And that special person yearn,
And to trust God learn.

When It Comes To Me

God doesn't play,
Because He answers and hears me when I pray.
I'm favored,
Because I will see the fruit of my labor.
God will come through and bless,
Even though I'm not perfect and I can be a hot mess.
I will manifest,
Because God said it's for me to have the best.
God sees my heart,
Because He is my everything, beginning and ending,
and He is how my day starts.
I've waited so I won't be in this situation for long,
Because God sees that my faith in Him is strong.
What I write and say don't doubt,
Because with my gifts and talents God is speaking through me
to let you know that He is an on-time God and not just in my
life but also in yours He is about to show up and show out.
God always smile,
Because I think about and do for others than myself,
so mercy and grace on me He piles.
God is pleased that I'm humble, grateful, faithful,
and thankful for so many reasons,
That's why I'm walking into my winning season.
God made me rare,
Because my light shines and love I'm
always willing to give and share.
So you better stay connected to me and you will witness and see,
That God is on point when it comes to me.

Shavetta Craig

Same God

Today, tomorrow, yesterday, and forever,
Will disappoint us never.
Who can heal the sick,
And by our side He will stick.
That brought others out,
He will do it for us so don't doubt.
That use David to do ministry,
Can use us too to bring forth His victory.
That delivered that woman with the issue of blood,
Can favor us as He did with Noah during the flood.
From generations before,
Can repeat the miracles and even do so much more.
Who created you, created me,
And light there was because He said let there be.
That did and showed signs and wonders
that seemed to be strange,
He is still doing that now He will never change.
That told the disciples and people back then
to have faith, trust, and believe,
Is that Savior now so we can receive.
That can still do the impossible now is doing
a continuous from back then,
We just need to be still and wait and
don't worry about the when.
That provided Moses with a staff and will
be our shield, amour, and rod,
So nothing is different, He is the same God.

So

Verily I say until you,
Ask, seek, and knock and the impossible will I do.
Be it,
And never lose faith and don't quit.
Let there be light and there was light,
And it will happen when the time is right.
Good to me,
Without Him where would I be.
Whosoever believe in Him shall not
perish but have everlasting life,
And shall be delivered from strife.
Be fruitful and multiply,
And on God rely.
Pick up your bed and go,
Because God said so.

Flawed But Favored

God uses me even in my strife,
To be a blessing in someone else's life.
My mistakes are my testimony to tell,
As in the presence of God I will dwell.
The failures and falls that try to define me,
I use it to do ministry.
Judging me don't do,
Because my trials and errors are what's going to help you through.
Scars you will see,
But I still have the victory.
I am an example of damage goods,
As God can cleanse and repair the mess under all of our hoods.
Challenges I still do face,
But faith I embrace.
I will be imperfect while living,
But God's glory, mercy, grace,
and love to me He is always giving.
I can still do God's work even if I'm taint,
Because a new image God can paint.
I have a past, history, and I have wronged and let others down,
But God saw in me a gem and turned my life around.
Even in my faults God still blessed me
and the miracles did not waiver,
I was chosen as I'm flawed but favored.

Abide

In God and Him in us,
As we are covered by the blood of Jesus.
In His will,
As it's for us to be still.
In faith, hope, and love,
And let God be first that we are thinking of.
In God's word,
And be doers of what we heard.
To God remain true,
And let faith guide you.
In God's presence dwell,
And we will have a testimony to tell.
By the promises God will keep,
And blessings we will reap.
In the thoughts, understanding, and ways God will provide,
So all we have to do is abide.

Endure

The challenges that you face,
Because your winning season you will embrace.
Through the storm,
Because when you least expect it miracles will form.
The heaviness of the pressure,
As God will bless you at all measures.
When you are down to empty,
Blessings you will reap plenty.
The wait,
Believe what God has for you is about to be great.
The uncomfortable position,
Because things in your life will transition.
The not having and lack,
Hold on because you are about to be
fruitful and gain everything back.
The not so nice,
Be still, I will never leave nor forsake you, and when the time
is right, I the Lord will make it happen are all God's advice.
The test,
Because you will manifest.
Trust the process because the impossible will happen for sure,
Because to reap, a famine, hardships, sufferings,
and difficulties you must endure.

A Walking Love Letter

Love is all me,
And through me it's for you to have and see.
I will continue to leave a residue,
Because it's for me to reach and touch you.
I will show you the meaning of letting go,
moving on, and how to forgive,
And how to heal so you can live.
What I offer is given freely and not rehearsed,
So carry it with you in your pocket and your
heart as I'm a form of a nurse.
I'm here to nurture,
As I'm the aide to be your suture.
Into your life I will pour,
And be a healing to the parts of your life
that is hurt, broken, and sore.
So much love, joy, and happiness I will spread,
To be that positive thought in your head.
I will motivate, encourage, inspire, comfort, and
support with my actions and with what I say,
And the answer when you pray.
Created to make your life, journey, and day better,
As God chose me to be a walking love letter.

Never Say Never

You are clueless to what you might do,
Because unforeseen circumstances you can go through.
The future you cannot predict or see,
So don't say that won't happen to me.
On others less fortunate don't frown upon or on them look down,
Because that could be you needing assistance to help
you back up and put back on your crown.
You might think you won't be in that
predicament or in a bad place,
You never know what you may have to face.
That you will not love again,
If you would wait and trust in God He will
send the one for your heart to mend.
Don't judge how another is trying to make it or getting by,
Because on you they surely can't rely.
The tables can always turn,
So let life be a lesson learned.
Put yourself in someone else's shoes,
Because you don't know the challenges, ups and downs, sacrifices,
and hardships they endured and even how they had to win to lose.
With what you have you are bless,
But there may come a time that you have less.
To have may not last forever,
So never say never.

It Was

Dead but now alive,
As things in your life will thrive.
Gone but given back,
You will be rewarded for your lack.
Lost but now found,
In your life God is turning things around.
Broken but now restored,
As love, joy, peace, and happiness will be on you galore.
Dark but found light,
Things are changing because the time is right.
Delayed but now on time,
The blessings and miracles are about to chime.
Stopped but now it will go,
So expect your increase, abundance, and overflow.
Weak but now strong,
And thank you for trusting and waiting
on God through the prolong.
Bad but now good,
Now things will happen in your life as it should.
Low but now high,
So on faith and hope rely.
Things will start getting better in your life just because,
As you stayed humble, faithful, grateful,
and thankful when it was.

Everything

Starts with having faith and in God trust,
And you will see miracles and the impossible form like dust.
Comes with a price,
And there must be a sacrifice.
Produce results from prayers,
Because for you God cares.
Happens when the time is right,
Because of your being still it brings God a delight.
Will suddenly and unexpectedly happen when you believe,
speak it, declare, decree, and claim,
And the blessings are coming for you they know your name.
Makes sense when on God you wait,
The manifestation will be great.
That was promised will be given to you,
It is your winning season so look at what God can and will do.
Will not come easy, have storms, troubles, tribulations, trials,
challenges, problems, and sufferings but there is an after a while,
And you be made perfect, establish, strengthen,
settle, and again you will smile.
Has a timing even though it tarry,
Someone will catch the vision and the assignment carry.
There is a coming through for what you went to God brings,
As God is the answer for everything.

Jesus Is Real

I don't care what you say,
Because He always comes through and answers when I pray.
For me His life He gave,
That's why today I'm saved.
The events in the Bible are nonfiction there is no act,
Jesus preformed every miracle and on us all He made an impact.
Because of Him I'm still here,
And that's why I walk by faith and not fear.
I am who I am because of the great I Am,
Who gets me out of any situation or jam.
Because what He did before, He will do now the same,
And He knows me by name.
So many storms He has brought me through,
And don't be silent because He did the same for you.
Whenever I ask, seek, and knock,
He was right on time when He wanted it
to happen it was never blocked.
Physically Him I can't see,
Because with my faith, trust, and wait I use my
spiritual eyes to see Him do the impossible, that's why
I can say He has been so good to me.
The sick, lame, and blind He heals,
So trust and believe that Jesus is real.

Open Doors

That I never would have expect,
And blessing me on all aspects.
That will lead to victory,
And I will give you all the credit, praise, and glory.
That no man can shut,
Because you save me every time God when I'm in a rut.
That I prayed for,
He exceeded my expectations and gave me so much more.
That seemed impossible,
Because nothing is too hard for God, He is able.
That I didn't see,
God is so good to me.
That has many with my name on it,
Because God favored me because I didn't lose faith or quit.
As I'm all yours,
As for me God you open doors.

I'm Just A Vessel

With gifts and talents to birth,
To serve a purpose here on earth.
For Gods use,
To be light and amuse.
That doesn't boast or take credit for anything,
Because my being and what I have and give
is because of God to me He brings.
To love and appreciate you,
And doing the assignment that God has for me to do.
To prove how good God is,
As the will and ways are all His.
Created from clay,
And trust in God every day.
Who serves a mighty Savior,
As He blesses me with favor.
I'm not perfect as at times with my flesh I wrestle,
But God still chose me as I'm just a vessel.

It's All God

You are just a vessel here on earth,
Doing what God was placed in you for you to birth.
You can't boost or take credit for anything,
Because all that you have God gives and brings.
Over your head is a roof,
And God keeps blessing you is the evidence and proof.
For all you have,
Even if little be humble, faithful, thankful, and
grateful so don't cry enjoy to laugh.
With you God always remain,
So don't grumble or complain.
You never would have made it this far,
So rejoice and be glad for who and whom you are.
Who kept you from what should have taken you out,
That is why you trust, believe, and have faith without the doubt.
It's God why you have breath, a job, shelter, and food,
So thank and praise Him for it, don't be rude.
Even with the troubles, storms, situations,
sufferings, and trials that you go through,
God is testing your faith and trust and then He will bless you.
Protection over you with favor, angels, the Holy
Spirit, amour, shield, staff, and rod,
That's why He comes first and He is the
only one because it's all God.

Be

The light that someone needs,
And be a reflection of God as you follow and He leads.
The water to help others grow,
And kindness and care show.
The cure to nurture,
And an aide to suture.
The listening ear when someone needs to vent,
And the rescue sent.
The support and ready to give,
While giving others a reason to want to live.
The comfort to sorrow and a broken heart,
And let your gifts and talents do their part.
The required peace,
And let your faith increase.
The encouragement that others desire,
And be the defuse to the fire.
The inspiration to the lost and weak,
And the gentleness, compassion, and serenity others seek.
The love that will sustain,
And that friend or companion remain.
The joy that others see,
These things and more for others be.

Shavetta Craig

It's Time To Rejoice

To be glad,
And focus on what's coming and not what you had.
Get ready to receive,
So believe.
It's coming your way,
So expect it any day.
The moment is for you,
The mind-blowing things God will do.
The wait is your comeback,
And you are getting back everything that you lack.
Things that were dead will come alive,
And right on time the blessings will arrive.
God is doing big things,
And all the impossible He brings.
So lift up your hands and praise with your voice,
Because it's time to rejoice.

Because You Pray

Favor God gives you,
So expect Him to prove what He said He would do.
Faith is your guide,
And watch God provide.
Fruitfulness God to you will add,
So thank and praise Him and rejoice and be glad.
Flourish of blessings will manifest,
Because you were consistent and never
stop it's on the way your best.
Fountain of youth will be,
As longevity and excellent health, you will see.
Flow of miracles God will cast,
And love will sustain you and last.
Fulfillment will be yours,
As God blows your mind with the open doors.
Floods of increase is coming your way,
This is how God moves because you pray.

Sudden

There will be a shake,
And in your life God will make a break.
You will see a change,
And it's not out of your range.
What you prayed and waited so long for,
Will show up unexpectedly and grant you want
you ask and then more.
It wasn't but instantly it is,
So trust and watch God because the timing is all His.
For all the going through,
As by surprise God will Himself or send someone to bless you.
You speak and it appears,
That's by faith and not fears.
A warning God will not give,
That's why He said get up and live.
In your life there will be a shift,
And don't be alarmed if it happens swift.
When you are going through and no matter
where you have been,
God will show up and show out all of a sudden.

We Need To Know

That you are God,
And that you are our protection with your
presence, staff, shield, amour, and rod.
That you are the only one,
To bless, save, carry, be there, and love us, so
God thank you for Jesus your Son.
That you are mighty and great,
And that you are worth the wait.
That our lives belong to you,
And the Holy Spirit is for us to accept and view.
That you we don't deserve,
But you we get to serve.
That us you are thinking of,
And us you love.
A plan for us you have,
And you want us to live life and laugh.
That when the time is right what's for us you will show,
Because you are the way we need to know.

The Reward Will Be Great

For all the struggles, hardships, and pain you had to go through,
God is surely going to bless you.
Great things take time so trust the process,
Even when it doesn't seem like it as you have
failures, learning lessons, falls, setbacks, delays,
and your life a mess.
You were planted to grow,
And in your winning season you will sow.
God is always on time and never late,
So what's for you expect and anticipate.
Having and walking in faith is the only way,
And you will see God when you trust and pray.
Nothing will ever come easy or just be handed to you,
Work and sacrifice you will have to do.
As hallelujah, thank you Jesus, and nobody but
God you will shout,
As in your life God will blow your mind
and show up and show out.
Just continue to wait,
Because right on time the reward will be great.

It's Hard To See

Outside the storm,
But miracles God will form.
What God is doing,
So in your faith keep pursuing.
What's on the way,
Continue to wait, trust, and pray.
Why you are going through,
Because something great is going to happen for you.
The winning season,
As your testimony will be for the right reason.
To finish the race,
You will get there by Gods mercy and grace.
The good out of this,
It will make sense and the reward you won't miss.
The blessings and victories for thee,
As sometimes it's hard to see.

Your Chariot Awaits

*You have been through more than enough battles,
storms, sufferings, troubles, and circumstances to
overwhelm that should have taken you out,
But even when it was so much easier to do,
you in your faith you didn't doubt.
You persevered and stayed strong for so many years,
You even kept smiling to fight back the tears.
For others you continue to be there,
Even when some didn't deserve it you still killed
them with kindness and showed love and care.
When you endured some unbearable bleeds,
You continue to put others first to be an inspiration,
encouragement, comfort, and support to their needs.
You watched many who didn't deserve become bless,
But you being who you are still cheered and was happy and
congratulated them even while you were in a mess.
So many broken pieces you have,
But you still say thank you God and continued to laugh.
From your ups and downs,
You will be gifted your crown.
All of this was not for nothing,
You believed it but you don't see that God is up to something.
No matter what you went through you looked beyond,
And for that of you God is fond.*

So count it all joy,
The enemy tried but he failed because what's attached to you
and what's for you, he is not a challenge for it, he can't destroy.
You have made it this far, so it's your time and season to win,
So because of your trust and faith in God
you, He has not forgotten.
God is saying that it's your turn,
And everything that you prayed, asked, seek,
and knocked for you will earn.
Your name is called and your blessings
have come now you are the bait,
So rejoice because your chariot awaits.

It's Done

The assignment God placed in my hand,
Why it took so long now you can understand.
So much was within me to birth,
To help so many here on earth.
My poetry was purposed just for each one of you,
As being your first aid kit was the challenge,
I was willing to do.
In each pages a message from God it sends,
As it gives you the strength for your hurt and pain to mend.
I brought clarity to the pollution,
As my words served as a solution.
My love was a need,
To stop your bleed.
I was a healing to your scorn,
Now you can move on.
Your brokenness can no longer predict your future,
As the words through these pages are your sutures.
As my poetry brought light to you as the sun,
Thank you for allowing me to be your rescue
as the assignment, it's done.